Arvind Krishna Mehrotra

Collected Poems

By the Same Author

Arvind Krishna Mehrotra

Collected Poems

Shearsman Books

Published in the United Kingdom in 2022 by
Shearsman Books Ltd
PO Box 4239
Swindon
SN3 9FN

Shearsman Books Ltd Registered Office
30–31 St. James Place, Mangotsfield, Bristol BS16 9JB
(this address not for correspondence)

www.shearsman.com

ISBN 978-1-84861-796-4

This volume was first published as *Collected Poems* by Giramondo Publishing, Sydney, in 2016, which in turn was an expanded version of *Collected Poems 1969–2014*, published by Penguin Books India in 2015. The present volume contains some extra poems and translations and some minor revisions.

for Vandana and Palash

ACKNOWLEDGEMENTS

The original copyright for the poems of Nirala, Shakti Chattopadhyay, Vinod Kumar Shukla, Pavankumar Jain and Mangalesh Dabral vests with the individual poets and their heirs.

Some of the new poems, uncollected poems, and uncollected translations first appeared in the following magazines and anthologies, to whose editors grateful acknowledgement is made: *Almost Island, Asian Literary Review, The Baffler, The Bombay Review, Bengal Lights, Both Sides of the Sky: Post-Independence Indian Poetry in English* (ed. Eunice de Souza), *The Common, Chandrabhāgā, Fulcrum, Granta, The Greenfield Review, Kavya Bharati, kayak, Memory's Gold: Writings on Calcutta* (ed. Amit Chaudhuri), *Poetry Wales, Shenandoah, Spoon River Poetry Review, Two Lines: Some Kind of Beautiful Signal* (eds. Natasha Wimmer and Jeffrey Yang).

I should like to thank Jyotirmoy Datta for providing me with literal line-by-line translations of Shakti Chattopadhyay's Bengali poems, and Ashok Vajpeyi, then in Bhopal, for making the exercise possible. The Gujarati poems of Pavankumar Jain were translated with the help of Vandana Jain and Jyotsna Milan. A residency at the Rockefeller Foundation's Bellagio Center helped me start on new poems and return to those already begun.

The excerpts from *The Absent Traveller* (1991, 2008) are reprinted here with the kind permission of Ravi Dayal Publisher and Penguin Books India, and the excerpts from *Songs of Kabir* (2011) with the kind permission of Hachette-Black Kite.

Contents

FROM MIDDLE EARTH (1984)

UNCOLLECTED POEMS 1985–1995

THE TRANSFIGURING PLACES (1998)

New Poems

TRANSLATIONS

UNCOLLECTED TRANSLATIONS

NIRALA

Author's Note

Just as some children when they grow up want to become snake charmers or railway engine drivers, I wanted at seventeen when I started writing to become a book. Not any book but a volume in, say, the Arden Shakespeare, or one in the uniform edition in the works of Walter Scott. The latter held particular appeal because it covered from end to end an entire shelf of my uncle's library, the books standing to attention like a platoon of soldiers in green jackets with gold buttons. A part of one shelf had the look of colourful bolts of fabric in a shop display. These were issues of *Poetry* magazine that arrived regularly once a month from Chicago, their single-coloured covers pink, red, blue, yellow, and green, and carrying a drawing of a winged horse. My uncle taught English at the University of Allahabad and the magazine came as a gift from the Americans, who were promoting American literature at Indian universities. Other bookshelves were as dull looking as a stack of bricks. These would be lined with the sturdy volumes of the Oxford World's Classics, or, more appropriately clad, those of Macmillan's *English Men of Letters* series that had rust spines. Some books seemed so old that I would not have been surprised to see them in a museum, kept there with other museum artefacts like terracottas and Roman silver coins. And then there were books whose look I disliked. They seemed ill, their skin grey, the paper inside yellow, the typeface heavy. I would take them out and hurriedly return them to the shelf, as though I had touched something that belonged more to a morgue than to a bookcase. One such book was Tagore's *One Hundred Poems of Kabir*. The edition I saw was from the 1940s, and there was hardly a year in the previous two decades when it had not been reprinted.

Memory is like a mirror. You blow on it and mist forms, then disappears. You have to keep blowing. The room full of books was part of a bungalow, and the bungalow, painted a dark red with white trim, had an address: 20 Hastings Road, Allahabad. It had gateposts, a circular drive bordered by a tall hedge, a wide verandah, a porte-cochère, in which a grey 1947 Opel Olympia was parked. My uncle, Kewal Krishna, whenever he had to get into the car was helped by the driver. He could not do it on his own. The driver would lift him from the wheelchair, which had been brought alongside the car, and deposit him in the front seat, then adjust his legs. The wheelchair was folded and went in the rear. To get out of the car the same process was repeated in reverse. It made for an unusual sight in a provincial town and there were always a few people who'd gather to see what was going on. My uncle had multiple sclerosis.

I was an undergraduate and lived with him and my aunt, Phyllis. She was English and they met when he was at Oxford in the early 1930s, where he wrote a dissertation on Horace Walpole and the English novel. They fell in love and got married. She came to India with him and though she lived into her nineties she went back to England only once, when her father died. Her father had a small business in High Street, and though I was only nine years old at the time I remember that she inherited some money. Some of it went in renovating the bungalow. The barbed wire fence that enclosed the compound was replaced with a boundary wall, and the thunderboxes with toilet seats. My aunt's surname was Ravenscroft, and I once came across a thick book, bound in red cloth and embossed with the Ravenscroft family crest, in which she had neatly updated the last page, adding her name, my uncle's, and my cousins', three girls, to the family tree.

The bungalow was built along the pattern of most colonial bungalows of the period: a living and dining room, flanked by rooms on either side, two on each. These rooms had smaller rooms attached to them, some used as dressing rooms. Except the smaller rooms, all the others had high ceilings and skylights, to which were fastened long cords, so that the skylights could be opened and closed. I occupied one of the smaller rooms, that was still large enough to accommodate a chest of drawers, a bed, a writing table and chair, and a bookrack. The window looked on to a row of oleanders that in the rainy season bore yellow flowers. Behind it were some old neem trees with thick trunks.

As you entered the living room from the verandah, the first room on the right was my uncle's library. It was called the study. This was where, sitting in an upholstered easy chair, breathing the fragrance that was a mixture of old paper, dust, and the dim light of a single 40-watt electric bulb, I spent most of my time. I'd look at the titles I was so familiar with and dream of a sleepy-eyed wide- hipped girl who was in school with me. The school was in Bhilai, a steel town in central India where my father, a dentist, had taken up a job. One day, sitting in the easy chair, I wrote my first poem. It was a poem of adolescent love, but it had a steady beat, which I only later recognised as iambic. I then wrote another. At the end of a few weeks I had enough for a small book. I typed them up on my Royal typewriter, one to a page as the poems were short, and took the sheets to a bookbinder in Colonelgunj, whose one-room establishment I passed on my way to the university. He had a round face and puffy eyes and was always dressed in a dhoti and vest. He was sitting cross-legged on the floor, surrounded by stacks of sheets, some of them folded and kept in another stack. There was a hand operated paper-cutting machine in one corner. Books in various stages of binding were in a shelf built into the wall. There were a couple of rolls of cloth, red, blue, lying around. Beside him, on a piece of paper, was a lump of glue, greenish white in colour and made from rice. I handed him the sheets I'd brought and we decided on the size, four and a half inches by six. He'd bind it in boards and asked me to choose the cloth. I chose blue; not Oxford blue but close. He told me to come back the next day.

I laid the book on my table and switched on the lamp. The binding was on the top so it opened like a note pad, but inside was a title page, a page of contents, a preface, followed by about 20 poems. Compared to the luxury liners in my uncle's library – the hardback volumes of the English poets printed in double columns – my vessel was not even a paper boat. I felt utterly defeated. It was terrible.

A book of poems, Wallace Stevens famously said, is a damned serious affair. Gathering the work of almost fifty years, the seriousness aside, is also damned difficult. It is difficult not so much because you cannot decide what to include and what to leave out, though there's some of that too, but because the itch to revise what was written decades ago can be irresistible.

Letting bygones be bygones, I have not, except occasionally, interfered too much with the text of previously published poems. In one poem I have changed the title: 'Eleven Cross-Sections' has here become 'Songs of the Good Surrealist', which is what it was called originally. For me who started writing in the 1960s, the discovery of surrealism helped resolve the awful contradiction between the world I wanted to write about, the world of dentists and chemist shops, and the language, English, I wanted to write in. Its music filled my ears and I could hear its 'soft inland murmur' as though it came from the leaves of the neem trees outside the window when the wind passed through them, and I could feel the slow beat of 'The still, sad music of humanity' on my pulse – but how does one write about an uncle in a wheelchair in the language of 'Tintern Abbey' or of skylarks and nightingales? It's as if I'd said to myself that since I cannot write about these things in English, let me do so in French, so to speak. Though I gave up trying to write like a surrealist long ago, there's no harm in acknowledging that I was a supporter of the party once. There's no harm in acknowledging either that those sweet-sounding birds, that I'd never before seen or heard, gave to the English language the mysterious attraction of a veiled face.

Before my discovery of the surrealists there had been another. In August 1965, as Wordsworth made way for Tennyson in the university English course and 'The Solitary Reaper' for 'Break, Break, Break', I came across *Penguin Modern Poets 5*. Though I would occasionally flip through the issues of *Poetry* magazine on my uncle's shelves, the American speech I now heard in the Penguin selection seemed closer to *our* everyday English in Allahabad than anything I'd read before. Here was Ginsberg's 'America' ('Go fuck yourself with your atom bomb'), Ferlinghetti's 'Underwear' ('Women's underwear holds things up / Men's underwear holds things down'), and Corso's 'Marriage' ('And should I then ask / Where's the bathroom?'). When together with Amit Rai, with whom I started the mimeographed little magazine *damn you* and who died the following year of leukemia, I first read these poems, neither of us could stop laughing, which is not how we responded to the great Romantics and Victorians, the explications of whose poems we had to mug up for our exams.

My subjects did not lie in England, France, or the United States, but I had to make a detour to those places, through their literatures, to realise, first, that my subjects lay nearer home, if not at home, and, second, to find a language in which to write about them. There still remained the question of how. The answer, set down as series of aphorisms, came from Ezra Pound's 'A Few Dont's by an Imagiste'. 'Go in fear of abstractions' said one of them. To someone like myself who had heard of Indian guru waffle and experienced some of it first hand, the aphorism seemed particularly appropriate. To complete the circle, the 'Dont's' had first appeared in the same *Poetry* magazine that I had looked at a little uncomprehendingly in my uncle's library.

Among my early poems, none of which are included here, were 'i am a farmer' published in *Manhattan Review* ('A Little Magazine of Emerging Poetry and Fiction') and 'The Private Ejaculations of Lord Krishna' in *The San Francisco Keeper's Voice* ('As of this publication, the *S.F. Keeper's Voice* will be published irregularly, i.e., whenever time, money, material, and mood are present simultaneously'). *Woodcuts on Paper* (1967), my attempt at concrete/visual poetry, for I could be a surrealist one day and quite a different creature the next, was a chapbook brought out by Gallery Number Ten, London. Despite its small 4" x 5" format, miminalist cover, and overall design, 24 loose sheets held together by a red slide binder, it was, to my eager eyes, a regular book.

By the time I was 20, then, I saw myself as less a student pursuing an MA degree in English at Bombay University, which is where I now was, and more as an established poet, published in London, New York, San Francisco, and Five Dock NSW. I was living in Deep Mandap, Agra Road, Mulund, Bombay, and from there travelled to Churchgate by local train for my classes.

As Bombay's suburban stations went by – Bhandup, Vikhroli, Ghatkopar, Kurla, Sion, Matunga, Dadar – I would have muttered, to the rhythm of their names but under my breath, the names of those foreign cities. 'The carnivorous train / swooped onto the platform' began a poem titled 'Dadar, Bombay'. It appeared in 1967 in *Poetry Australia*. When it came to the landscape of poetry, I was, in my mind, living elsewhere. Four years later, in 1971, I found myself in the Midwest, at the University of Iowa's International Writing Program, where that self-image underwent a severe correction. It was far easier, I realised, to be an American poet in Allahabad than to be an Indian-born American poet in Iowa City. I returned to India in 1973, and except for one brief trip abroad did not leave India again for the next 23 years.

The poems are arranged chronologically: Uncollected Poems 1972–74, *Nine Enclosures* (1976), *Distance in Statute Miles* (1982), *Middle Earth* (1984), Uncollected Poems 1985–95, *The Transfiguring Places* (1998), and New Poems. The chronological ordering, however, is a little deceptive. *Middle Earth*, for instance, was a selection, drawing on the two books that preceded it, *Distance in Statute Miles* and *Nine Enclosures*. But it also had a group of new and uncollected poems, a few of the latter, as the dates below them indicate, written as early as 1972. Also written in 1972 is 'Fantomas', which appears in the first section here, Uncollected Poems 1972–74. Initially, it was part of the 'Good Surrealist' poems, but then got detached from the sequence and was published independently. The poems in Uncollected Poems 1985–95 were meant to appear in *The Transfiguring Places* but did not. They were suppressed in what must have been a moment of poetic doubt, and happy though I am for the doubt to lift, I wish I could recall what particular aspect of the poems made me suppress them in the first place. The New Poems of the concluding section were written over the last sixteen years or so.

A little less than a third of the book consists of translations. Selections from *The Absent Traveller* (1991) and *Songs of Kabir* (2011) are followed by modern Indian poems translated from three languages, Hindi (Nirala, Vinod Kumar Shukla, Mangalesh Dabral), Gujarati (Pavankumar Jain), and Bengali (Shakti Chattopadhyay). Some of the Nirala poems have previously appeared in *Distance in Statue Miles*, but the others are collected here for the first time. Together, the translations cover a period from the first century CE to the present, and though that was never my intention, they, albeit with big gaps, tell the story of Indian poetry over two millennia. Whether it is in their own words or through a *persona*, those who do the telling seldom speak in whispers. To hear them on human sexuality or human folly is to hear our own voices, voices that we keep hidden from ourselves, finding them either too blunt or too cruel or too unfeeling. That's where the poets come in.

It was only a few years after I had started writing that I found myself doing translations. In the late 1960s Adil Jussawalla had been commissioned by Penguin to edit *New Writing in India*, the last book to appear in their New Writing series, and the earliest translations were made for him. But even before that I had tried my hand at redoing Kabir, not from Hindi but from existing English translations like Tagore's, though it was not Tagore's that I redid. That was done by Robert Bly. I must have picked up some other translation, and the desire to see Kabir's iconoclastic poems in a more contemporary English that captured the urgency of his speech and the directness that comes with it, led me to recast them. It was another 40 years before I figured out the right mould for the recast: the American idiom.

Sometime in the mid-1980s Arun Kolatkar in Bombay introduced me to the Prakrit poems of the *Gāthāsaptaśatī*. He was reading them in a Marathi translation, but since I knew neither Prakrit nor Marathi, nor Sanskrit and German, the other two languages into which the poems had been translated, I decided to make my own English versions, aided by a literal English translation, several dictionaries, and a patient tutor.

You translate in order to share with those who may not know the original the excitement of reading, the simple joys of literature as well as its privileges; and the more you desire to share the less exhaustible the pleasures seem. The ancient Prakrit poems appeared to have been written by Imagists from another tradition, two millennia before the Anglo-American phenomenon. Much is left unsaid in them, and yet everything that could be said about the man-woman relationship, particularly the sexual relationship, was said. Pound's note to one of the poems in *Cathay*, 'The Jewel Stairs' Grievance', could stand as a gloss to a Prakrit verse:

Jewel stairs, therefore a palace. Grievance, therefore there is something to complain of. Gauze stockings, therefore a lady, not a servant who complains. Clear autumn, therefore he has no excuse on account of weather. Also she has come early, for the dew has not only whitened the stairs, but has soaked her stockings. The poem is especially prized because she utters no direct approach.

The poems of the Beats, those of Kabir, and, further back, those of Prakrit poets who sang of unfaithful husbands and unfaithful wives, treating it as norm rather than exception, came to be linked in my mind. The thread joining them was transgression. In the poem from *Cathay*, it was probably a married man who failed to keep his appointment with the lady in gauze stockings.

From time to time I would be drawn to the work of modern poets, some from languages – Gujarati, Bengali – I did not myself know. Here again, I took the help of others. The reason I translated their poems was the frisson I felt on reading them or as they were read to me, and as with the Prakrit and Kabir, the frisson was repeated the moment I reimagined them in English. You can be as strongly drawn to a poem as you would be to another person.

The poets are varied in style, form, and tone, but except for Nirala occasionally, their language, their version of 'plain American which cats and dogs can read', does not call attention to itself. What calls attention is the trepidation with which they approach the world, as though they did not wish to disturb its arrangement, and the starkness of their vision as they reconfigure it. In 'Breaking stones', in which Allahabad is called by its modern name for the first time in Hindi poetry (its ancient name is Prayag), Nirala sees a common enough sight, a woman breaking stones by the road, but when she meets his gaze her eyes 'spoke of pain / But not defeat.' In 'This year too in the plains', Vinod Kumar Shukla shuffles Indian cities around, changing the map of the country, but only at the end of the poem do we see why he's being so playful. Similarly, in 'This colourful picture' a lower middle class man, a father, brings home a picture of chubby-faced children, but there's anxiety written on his face. Pavankumar Jain realises in middle age that he's never stepped out of a stroller, that his parents have robbed him of his life as much as given it. Both he and Mangalesh Dabral, when they look around, at the interiors of rooms and outside the houses they live in, notice things that other people would notice too – a tattered shopping bag, grass, squirrels, a ball – except that self-absorbed other people hardly notice their shopping bags, tattered or not, especially when empty. And in 'It's Not a Very Happy Time' Shakti Chattopadhyay walks into a tottering surreal tower of images as he makes his way home after another night of drinking.

Odd as it may seem, there have been Indian poets – Toru Dutt, A. K. Ramanujan, Dilip Chitre – who have devoted as much time to translation as to their own poems. In Toru Dutt's case, who translated mainly from the French, the number of her translations greatly exceeds the number of her original poems. I do not know what conclusion to draw from this, except that when it comes to the labour required of you, the roles of poet and translator are indistinguishable from each other.

ARVIND KRISHNA MEHROTRA
JULY 2016

Uncollected Poems

1972–1974

Fantomas

She went never to return
She went and her twisted arm entered
A length of intestine came in through the skylight
She sent a steaming cauldron in which she'd cooked her nails
Her toe whizzed past
Then her button with a piece of thread attached like a tail
Then a whole eyelash
Her short hair bounced into the room, a black rabbit
Her nose hopped erratically, looking for its twin
Greetings from her armpits' two tiny hedgehogs
Her leg beams from outer space

1972

Three Questions for Prabhu S. Guptara Concerning his Anthology of Indian Religious Poetry in English

I
Dear Mr Guptara,
The day I got your letter
I'd had myself vaccinated against smallpox.
Do you think the vaccination will rise?

II
Dear Mr Guptara,
I washed my shirt this morning
and it's still wet round the collar.
Do you think the earth is pear-shaped?

III
Dear Mr Guptara,
For heaven's sake.
But then that girl in red
bicycling down the road,
isn't she so utterly religious.

Ballad of the Black Feringhee

I would rather sing folk songs against injustice
and sound like ash cans in the early morning
or bark like a wolf
from the open doorway of a red-hot freight
than sit like Chopin on my exquisite ass.
                              —Carl Rakosi

India it is midnight the tenth of March and I open my palm
India the silver coin doesn't vanish, the matchbox doesn't fly into
      the trees, and I pick the wrong jack
India I've hung up my magician's gloves
India I've been betrayed by the tricks learnt in the long narrow
      rooms of Allahabad, Ljubljana, and Iowa City
India I've returned to the brightness of your streets,
      the regularity of your sounds, the evenness of your days
India I'm going to hypnotise your bricks
India listen to the grass, there's something going on in Ethiopia
India give me five pounds of rice and I won't ever leave
India give me a peanut and I'll shut my window
India my hands are tied and my footprints trapped like wild pigeons
India what are the first principles of ventriloquy
India I was born in the year of your independence
India I've been trying to procure a bottle of kerosene
India what will I do when the lights go out
India if you blindfold me I'll see you better
India will I always have to write in the dark
India the cats are nervous
India where's my horoscope
India you were an astrological mistake
India I'm afraid of your truckers, shopkeepers, postmen, and herbs
India the man in the street is a shrewd animal
India you don't transport them in trains

India you don't tie them to trees and shoot them
India you kill them in 'encounters'
India you kill them while they're trying to 'escape'
India your police stations are little Siberias
India when they come for me I'll put on a clean shirt
India their bullets won't settle on me like flies
India I want to wrap you in an old newspaper and carry you from door
    to door
India there's no need to hide your large teeth
India what a big nose you have
India remember the pile of ash on Mandelstam's left shoulder
India don't destroy yourself in slow motion

1974

Nine Enclosures

(1976)

Between Bricks, Madness

I
Must make a poster
march with workers to the factory
straighten my eye with a hammer
Get a jack
raise my flat voice
replace my nose with a sickle

And another palm
is transferred
to my hand

II
Must pick up an axe
reach the forest
chop down an elder tree

Move steadily on my raft
burn myself
at every port

Turn into stranger
make a quick bed
of skyline and straw

Or just sit by the window playing dice
my bow bigger than my arrow

Let my even mind clap on the shore as the river runs on

III
The bookcase and inkwell
the replicas of swords
come between us

My mother wasn't opened
by a midwife's finger
the hyena didn't clean out my cradle

I didn't take the stone's advice
on locusts
feel the earth like a trench

And still want to lead
my twenty-year-old
toy frigates into battle

IV
I cannot be
graceful as the beast

nibble like a mouse
mate heavily like the bull

be flying insects
born under lamp posts, buried in air

or birds
whose continents are the seasons

or fish
whose national border
is no fisherman's net

or night
which brings
the dialects together

or swamp
which hides the rhino's horn
the poacher's shoe

or winter
which sits on the pane
a freezing butterfly

I cannot be leaf or water
hillside or seabed
mule or star

V
It is written
'When the cloud signals
when the curse around the moon is lifted
when lightning falls with the calmness of rain
when memories rub like branches
on roofs of deserted summer houses
when the long snow melts and they
resume the hunt for the yeti
when the storm bends and touches
when the new seed opens its palm
when stone-snakes recover their poison

wind its fearlessness
water its frenzy
when insects narrate the changes in weather
when a naked man
a flat-eyed goat on his back
dances upon the steps of sunset'

Songs of the Ganga

I
I am Ganga
Snow from the mountains
The keeper of water

I am the plains
I am the foothills
I carry the wishes of my streams
To the sea

I am both man and woman

I am paper boats for children
I am habits for fishermen
I am a cloud for shaven monks
I reflect all movement

I am the bridge
I am the fort and the archer
Taking aim
I am the great dissolver of men

I give life and I take it back

II
I go out into the world
I am the world
I am nations, cities, people
I am the pages of an unbound book

My room is the air around me

I am dressed in water
I am naked as water
I am clarity

A friend comes along
Offers me a flag
And says a government has fallen

I'm going to catch rain, I say
And spread out a net

I am poison

III
Billy goats
Come down from the mountain
Without finding solitude
Camels return from the desert

I make two lines in the sand
And say they are unbreakable walls

I make the four directions one
I know the secret of walking

I am the death of fire

IV

From smoke I learn disappearance
From the ocean unprejudice

From birds
How to find a rest house
In the storm

From the leopard
How to cover the sun
With spots

In summer I tend watermelons
And in flood I stay
Near the postman's house

I am a beggar
I am a clown
And I am shadowless

The Sale

I
It's yours for the price, and these
old bits have character too. Tomorrow
they may not be available.
Naturally I can't force you
to buy them, and were I not leaving
– you heard the sun choke on an eclipse? –
I would never have thought of selling.
You take your time though, and
satisfy yourself. This is Europe,
that America, this scarebug Asia,
that groin Africa, an amputated
Australia. These five. I don't have more.
May be another egg-laying island remains
in the sea. You remember in my letter
I wrote of forests? Here they are,
wrapped in leaves, and carrying
them shouldn't be difficult.
This skull contains the rivers.
About that I'm sorry. Had you come
yesterday I could have given you two.
I'll take another look. Yes, I did
have a mummy somewhere. Just last night
the pyramids came
and knocked at my gate for a long time.

II
Would you mind if I showed you
a few more things?
Be careful, one river is still wet
and slippery; its waters continue to
run like footprints. Well, this is
a brick and we call that string.
This microscope contains the margins
of a poem. I've a map left, drawn
by migrating birds.
Come into the attic.
That's not a doll – it's the photograph
of a brain walking
on sand and in the next one
it's wearing an oasis-like crown.
I must also show you a tiger-skin
that once hid a palace.
On one roof you'll see
the antelope's horns,
on another the falling wind. These round
things are bangles and that long one
a gun. This cave is the inside
of a boot. And here
carved wheels turn through stone.

III
I wish you had asked me earlier.
The paintings have been bought
by a broken mirror
but I think I can lead you
to a crack in the wall.
I've a skeleton too.
It's full of butterflies
who at dawn will carry away
the crown.
I've also a wheelchair to show you.
It belonged to my uncle,
and one day the hook
that hangs from the sky
touched him. If you open the cupboard
you'll see his memory
on the upper shelf and two books
now yours:
Ruskin's *Lectures on Art*
and *A Short History of English Literature* by Legouis.
I'll take another minute.
Can you climb this ladder?
Well, that's the sun and moon
and with this candle you can
work the clouds. I'm sorry I was
short of space
and had to pack the Great Bear
in this clock. Oh them,
let them not worry you.
They're only fisherman and king,
who will leave soon as one's bait
is ready and the other's dominion.

Songs of the Good Surrealist

I
The air folds, a sheet of paper
Countries turn in the wind as feathers
Maps run aground
Toys, globes, tugs, bob in the sea
Everything looks alike to the sky
On a shoreless earth a war of colours
Nothing changes

II
Talking of animals I've seen cats
Sulking beside the sea

There lies at its bottom
A submarine full of mice

III
A coin, a small fire, a handkerchief
A drop, a wooden elephant, a leaf
A storm, a passage for glaciers, a bowl

Fire has the smell and colour of lemons
The elephant brings down rain with his trunk
The glacier rolls on its side and dies

Hair the length of stars
One eye cocoon, other hive
Ears more luminous than spiders

IV
Mountains, nomads, undisturbed children, kings
Walked the continents
Hunted for their sacred features
Odd habits, perfect skulls
Some died, some fell into rivers
Some returned quickly to the earth

Footprints still lead from cave to cave
A small black lake where he may have stood

V
Lines on my palm, fish in an aquarium

VI
When two stones, two branches rub
We have fire
Each time a man is forgotten
There's a tremor
The sky gets crowded with balloons
Prayers and mushrooms
Animals and clowns are the forgeries of dreams

VII
Inside an abandoned trunk
Hands, feet
A portion of a head

The hands belong to a dead mason
The left foot to an escaped prisoner

The head sits on the table
And doesn't say a word

VIII
Clouds cannot always be trusted
This one broke into my house
Went behind the cupboard, barked

I left the city
And like any hunting dog
It picked up the scent

IX
Looking at fruit ripens them
The apple turns brown in an hour
The milk tooth enters a wish
Mornings I fell from trees are poisoned wells
I run out of a silver gate
A serpent's hood is on the curtain
And breathing near the wall my sister's murderer

X
I swallowed a round minute
Fed clocks to my sheep
Tied them to the wings of birds
Burnt them in fireplaces
Dissolved them in chemicals
Sent them away in ships I knew would sink
Only to be shown by the round head of a flower
The soil's mechanism

XI

Trees drop their weapons
Announcing truce
And the encircled crow
Grows a secret feather

Just where the valley
Spreads out another sun
The blue sky turns into shades of grey
The mind rolls down a flat mountain

The Book of Common Places

I
The kiln isn't far from here
And in the east
A little travelling remains.
My companions are a thimble,
A bottle of water,
A first aid kit,
Tobacco,
One page from a logbook,
And five directions
In each hand.

In the square
Two dolls
Are being tried.
I never begin a journey
On a Thursday.

II
The eyes don't seem
Well at all.
They smell like exhausted tea leaves
And drop objects.
Lying in bed I hear
The rocker
Hit the same spot on the wall
And wonder how the rain feels
When it is measured
In inches.

In the photograph
Everyone wears a striped
Blazer, and tennis racquets
Are crossed like knives
In the foreground.

III
Land
And sea routes,
Trade winds
And cold deserts,
Inscriptions
On tombs and coins,
Settle down
Like particles of salt.
My dreams have the colour
Of early morning.

The old lioness
Stands in the window
And waves
To the Sunday crowd.
A child starts crying.

IV
The white room
Is tied like a bandage
Around me.
This was a quiet
Neighbourhood,
Known only to journeymen

And migrant saints,
Before the inventors
Of steam
Moved in.

Dressed in his cap
And belt,
The beggar of the city
Walks down the road
Like a dying planet.

V
In a glass jar
The unnatural foetus
Is preserved
Like a find.
My hand is cursive
And illegible
In winter.
The Pied Piper returns
To his cave
In the hills.

The thief
Admires the house
From the road
And leaves without stepping
On the cobbles.

VI
The bat
Came in
Through the window.
I see it dying
In equal pieces
And don't have the strength
To touch
Its wings.
My voyage
Has just begun.

The little boy
Explains
Why more and more birds
Keep refusing
To cross the equator.

VII
The widow next door
Lives off her trained
Parrot.
It reads the future
And tells you when
To avoid it.
At night
She dances in the trees
And fills the air
With abuse.

The decorated general
Is alone

In his tent;
The pyres burn
Like new volcanoes.

VIII
From outlying districts
Goldsmith
And tanner
Arrive by boat.
We sit around
Talking of simple
Believable things.
I show them my new pair of ampersands
And notice they're singing
Last year's songs.

The fish
Wishes it were
An illustration
In a book
Of symbols.

IX
The letterbox
Is the captain of my street
And a good acquaintance
Of the lighthouse.
Once in a while
We get together
And change
The altitude of stars.

The cold current turns red,
The warm one blue.

The soldier, returning
From furlough, checks
His whistle and mug;
His son learns how to count
By watching trains.

X
Five shipwrecks make
One sailor.
I brought home the first pigeon
I shot
And hid it
Under a flowerpot.
A body of ants
Trooped by.
After this incident I took
Interest in limestone quarries.

For three months
The boats
Stay close together
And clouds
Huddle above the Arabian Sea.

XI
My childhood
Wanders off into the family tree,
And the tree gets lost

In the north.
I'm told we followed the tracks
Left by none in particular,
The horse
Was our animal,
And once in the plains
We settled among rivers.

Both prisoner
And guard
Notice
The squirrel's
Transparent leap.

XII
The shadowless tribesmen
Easily picked out the gaps
In the procession
Of mountains;
Then a few ships
Filled with white traders
Swung round the Cape
And sighted the west coast.
They redid the land
From sea to sea.

The numismatist
Calculates
The age of a coin;
The pigeons feed
From an old newspaper.

XIII

The simplest shapes remain
And it's time
To praise
What is left of my city:
The pleaders circling above,
A line of potters come to an end.
These are my incidents.
I depend on the rag-and-bottle man
And know nothing
About styles of architecture.

Yesterday
All the rare lines
In the book
Were traded
For common ones.

XIV

Not even the nine of diamonds
Can match the queen of spades
In cruelty.
The ageing scholar finds
His last book
Buried in the first.
I have one
More superstition.
It has to do
With custard-apples.

While the clown
Removes his makeup,
The trapezist
Stands
On air.

XV
She is about
To thread the needle
When a yellow butterfly distracts her.
I go upstairs,
Study the map, and move
The field guns
Near a clump
Of trees.
My toys
Are safe for children.

The artillery
Stops at the door
And turns back;
The ants quickly
Go over the horizon.

Index of First Lines

I
She is snake, she is wind, she is
Leaf, her cry is a knock
On the door and I let her enter.
Her face is like paper
On which something has been written
And erased many times. The door closes.
She sits in an armchair, leans
Forward, and gives me a ring of white hair.
She wants me to keep it
Till she calls again.
It's half-past four in the morning
And I'm still awake. The wedding music
Stops for a while. Whiteness
Returns to the walls.
Old woman, how can I be
Astonished by sunlight when it breaks
So evenly?
A condemned building
Cannot lean on its shadow.

II
She enters through a door
In the kitchen,
I pretend I'm asleep.
She sits at the foot of my bed,
And I notice her hands
Resemble her father's. It's past eleven.
The sun has risen despite the rain.
The birds get up
But stay close to their nests.
Soon it will be dark.
Inside my mouth
I see a farrier's anvil.
Old woman, tell me
Where adamant is found.
The birds' feet are tied,
They have chipped voices,
And I've sold my compass
For a clay medallion.

III

She is an elf, she is a wand, she is
A goblin. She comes as she pleases.
She no longer taps like the rain,
She stands in the window
Like sunset.
On Sundays she opens
A book of charts
And turns a page. I watch
The edges of a continent run
Into the colours of the sea.
Old woman, tell me about the death
Of mercury. Tonight I'll enter
Your mutable country
Where the land doesn't tighten
Over water like a shoe and the moon
Spills all its light
On the sky. I touch my words
And they rise to be near your empty hands.

Remarks of an Early Biographer

I

There was something there we had
Not known before, that he hadn't
Mentioned in rhyme, but our first job
Was to coax the ancient vase
Into letting us enter.
The dust hung in mid air,
The books he hadn't finished
Lived and waited in the walls,
His desk, when it saw us, raised
The drawbridge.
In all we spent three days
Expecting some bird, some omen,
To turn up another secret.
We came down the steps
Remembering we hadn't climbed them
To get there; we looked back
And the room had folded.

II

Then one summer day,
Just as the sun rose on its thin
Elbows, I returned, alone.
The lines in my pocket bore
A resemblance to ivory knives
And had the fresh smell of gunpowder.
On pane and mirror
I interpreted the shapes of light
And uncovered the route he took
To escape into the clean
Edges of the sky.
The river had aged, becoming
A serpent with invisible scales,
The old banyan tree slept,
Its head filled with roots,
And the women of the city asked,
Has he opened or closed the windows?

III

In his keen memory he stored
His silences like mistresses
And it isn't my intention
To disturb that symmetry of holes.
As I turn the pages of his notebook
A few characters come apart;
Once more I prod
The shallow vessel filled with ash,
Then return my guides to their frontiers:
The spider to the trellis,
The rat to the cupboard,
The lizard to the brick.
As a child he divided words
With a shaving blade, or turned them
Inside out like caps; at death,
His mouth was open, his right hand warm,
As if it had never written.

Genealogy

I

I recognise my father's wooden skin,
The sun in the west lights up his bald bones,
I see his face and then his broken pair of shoes,
His voice comes through, an empty sleeve.
Birds merge into the blue like thin strokes.
Each man is an unfinished fiction
And I'm the last survivor of what was a family.
They left in a caravan, none saw them
Slip through the two hands.
The dial spreads on the roof,
Alarms put alarms to sleep,
Led by invisible mules I take a path across
The mountains, my alchemies trailing behind
Like leather-bound nightmares.
There isn't a lost city in sight. The map I had
Preserved drifts apart like the continents it showed.

II

My shadow falls on the sun and the sun
Cannot reach my shadow. Near the central home
Of nomad and lean horse I pick up
A wheel, a migratory arrow, a numeral.
The seed is still firm. Dreams
Pitch their tents along the rim.
I climb Sugar Mountain,
My mother walks into the horizon,
Fire breaks out in the nests,
Trees, laden with the pelts of squirrels,
Turn into scarecrows,
The seed sends down another merciless root.
My alembic distils these fairy tales,
Acids, riddles, the danger in flowers.
I must never touch pollen or look
Into a watchmaker's shop at twilight.

III

My journey has been this anchor,
The off-white cliff a sail,
Fowl and dragons play near the shores
My sea-wrecked ancestors left.
I call out to the raven, 'My harem, my black rose,
The clock's slave, keeper of no-man's-land between us.'
And the raven, a tear hung above his massive pupil,
Covers my long hair with petals.
Only once did I twist the monotonous pendulum
To enter the rituals at the bottom of twelve seas,
Unghostlike voices curdled my blood, the colour
Of my scorpion changed from scarlet
To scarlet. I didn't mean to threaten you
Or disturb your peace I know nothing of,
But you – living in these fables, branches,
And, somehow, icebergs – tell me, whose seed I carry.

Continuities

I

This is about the green miraculous trees,
And old clocks on stone towers,
And playgrounds full of light
And dark blue uniforms.
At eight I'm a Boy Scout and make a tent
By stretching a bed sheet over parallel bars
And a fire by burning rose bushes,
I know half a dozen knots and drink
Tea out of enamel mugs.
I wear khaki drill shorts, note down
The number plates of cars,
Make a perfect about-turn for the first time.
In September I collect my cousins' books
And find out the dates of the six Mughals
To secretly write the history of India.
I see Napoleon crossing the Alps
On a white horse.

II

My first watch is a fat and silver Omega
Grandfather won in a race fifty-nine years ago;
It never works and I've to
Push its hands every few minutes
To get a clearer picture of time.
Somewhere I've kept my autograph book,
The tincture of iodine in homoeopathy bottles,
Bright postcards he sent from
Bad Ems, Germany.
At seven-thirty we are sent home
From the Cosmopolitan Club;
My father says No bid,
My mother forgets her hand
In a deck of cards.
I sit on the railing till midnight,
Above a worn sign
That advertises a dentist.

III

I go to sleep after I hear him
Snoring like the school bell;
I'm standing alone in a back alley
And a face I can never recollect is removing
The hubcaps of our Ford coupé.
The first words I mumble are the names of roads:
Thornhill, Hastings, Lytton.
We live in a small cottage,
I grow up on a guava tree,
Wondering where the servants vanish
After dinner, at the magic of the bearded tailor
Who can change the shape of my ancestors.
I bend down from the swaying bridge
And pick up the river
That once tried to drown me.
The dance of the torn skin
Is for much later.

from Distance in Statute Miles

(1982)

Lies

My pockets are empty
June, Peeks, and I
Marched together
On Annual Day
June had brown eyes and thin legs
Peeks was my only rival

My pockets
Like two secret chambers
Held tamarind seeds
Pieces of white chalk
And parts of a catapult
I had a dream this morning

Five blue whales
Rushed out of the sea
They stood up on the beach
They moved across the land
They turned towards me, tall
And smooth in the early light

I confuse dreams with lies
I was born with a thin snake
Coiled over my head
That snake was an amulet
That snake ate only pigeons
That snake spoke in my ear

Letter to a Friend

I set up the house while she waited
In another city, the day of our marriage
Was still far. When she saw the rooms
For the first time she said, 'These
Are worse than bathrooms.'
She found the walls too narrow and wanted
To run away; your mother and my aunt
Were both there when this happened.
Your mother in her enthusiasm
And simple joy
Asked us over for lunch
When she said, 'I know nothing of lunches.'
It was months before things got normal again.
Anyhow, she spent her first days
With the clear sky, a few birds, the little
Interesting things that gather
Around trees. We slept in the afternoon
And awoke when the long sad evening
Was already halfway up the window.
Kitchen smoke, the quiet smell
Of me reading in my chair, the glum
Books that smacked their tails
On the shelves like field-mice, the family
Downstairs quarrelling and crying,
Poisoned the tips of needles in her mind
And she entered an imprisoned kingdom –
A place I wouldn't touch with my bare hands.
Through two short rooms she walked
As if I were out to murder her last secret,
And a blackness we all feel took hold of me;

I wanted it to, to protect myself;
Her eyes glistened, scared, scary.
At night insects on wings and feet would come
To relieve the stiff air. We played
Under the sharp moon, making little noise
Since I hardly touched her.
The first caw and the excitement
Of crows as they looked at us in bed from the chimney,
Bees rushed into the room, the sun pulled up,
And the girl next door wrung her underwear;
She knew I admired her ankles even in sleep.
The milk-woman brought her dog with her,
The postman came up the steps and she spent
Hours reading letters from her family,
Then wrote to each one of her brothers and sisters.
The lama would knock and take off his shoes
Before entering. He would hold her hand and talk
Of silence, of living in the mountains
With just enough candles to scatter the dark.
We fetched water in metal buckets, cooked
In the open, and lying on the hillside
None thought of love.
She made tea by boiling
Water, leaves, milk, and sugar
Together, adding condiments in the end;
When he left, her palms were wet
And I wasn't jealous.
Across the clean flat roofs and narrow road
Is a bare field. A camel once sat there all day,
Thin legs folded under the hump,
Looking at cows walk through the trees.
So has it been.

Her blood has got more entangled in its stones,
While I've kept to my lamp, beads, mirrors, jars,
A rug, pictures of purple demons,
Red, black, and white ants, all sorts of fat spiders.
Three years, and I still wonder
What nakedness is, or does.
Sometimes I notice the couple next door.
It's very warm outside,
And the streets are tall and quiet.

Inland

There's no escape from this.
Birds, in twos, in threes,
Fly straight ahead,
Closing the sky behind them.
The walls of our house are damp
From last month's rain.

Kite

Summer is at hand.
New leaves fill the branches
With sunlight, a red and green kite
Bends into the wind. It is two bits
Of thin paper
Joined in the middle. It opens the sky.
I have three small rooms and a terrace
Where I sit out and read Han-shan
To my newborn son, or make
That kite. My possessions are few.
I'll stay here.

Canticle for My Son

The dog barks and the cat mews,
The moon comes out in the sky,
The birds are mostly settled.
I envy your twelve hours
Of uninterrupted dreaming.

I take your small palms in mine
And don't know what
To do with them. Beware, my son,
Of those old clear-headed women
Who never miss a funeral.

January

The gate wide open; chairs on the lawn;
Circular verandahs; a narrow kitchen;
High-ceilinged rooms; arches; alcoves; skylights.
My house luminous; my day burnt to ash.

October

Reconsider, first, the patch of light
Already there when you open
The door to a high-ceilinged room;
Then, halfway up the wall, the alcove
Filled with painted clay toys;
Above it, behind the skylight, a white
Moistureless cloud. Yes, the replenished hour
Illuminates the house; light heals the day.

Not Through Glass

The hills are across the border.
Birds scream and rain falls.
I listen to the pines
Talk of small animals afraid to go home,
High mountains keeping watch over valleys,
The wind gathering evidence.
Smoke rises from the middle of the forest
Like a quiet hunter.
The sea is a thousand miles away,
Tides push against the walls,
Tree bark and uncovered roots
Flicker like lights in the rain.
The air is chilly. The pines move into my room.

Engraving of a Bison on Stone

The land resists
Because it cannot be
Tempted, or broken
In a chamber. It records,
By carefully shuffling the leaves,
The passage of each storm, rain,
And drought. The land yields
In places, deliberately,
Having learnt warfare from the armies
It fed. The land is of one
Piece and hasn't forgotten
Old miracles: the engraving of a bison
On stone, for instance. The land
Turns up like an unexpected
Visitor and gives refuge, it cannot be
Locked or put away. The land
Cannot sign its name, it cannot die
Because it cannot be buried,
It understands the language,
It speaks in dialect.

Distance in Statute Miles

On maps it always takes
The same position: away from the coastline,
Two inches below
The mountain range. But the man
Who is turning the page doesn't know
That it is flat as a blade, more
Vulnerable than a child, inaccessible
By road or air. It is in front of me.
I can see the towers
From my window, I call out
And it responds to its name,
It is easily frightened.
This is a winter afternoon and the sun
Makes unequal rectangles
Of light in each courtyard, by evening
The birds will again be visible.
Far from us, near the river
That was once leased out to fishermen,
A small East German tractor is sending up smoke.

To a T'ang Poet

Late December afternoon,
I walk along Buxi Bund
Towards Nagabasuki on the edge of town.
The river has receded.
Undivided green fields on three sides.
Remote birds in the sky.
Wide steps and broken masonry.
A channel ahead.
Ducks paddling across it.

River Stop

Travelling alone
In the northern mountains,
I see the river
Rise along the banks,
Pick up a road or two.
Once or twice a year
It steps ashore
And looks back on the bridges
It missed.
The boats watch
From high ground.

Star, oar, and fish
Move across the window
Like three forgetful children.
I measure their sleeves
And make them
Little red coats,
I draw magic circles around them
So that they don't lose each other;
They disappear into the unlit hills.

The road to the river
Is lined with trees,
Where small groups
Of stone-faced pilgrims
Await transport.

Two Lakes

Lakes do not happen
Only in geography.
I know one with a fake Japanese garden
And a toy zoo. It is circled
With a red road and is completely
Artificial. Among its reflections
Are isolated trucks, fragrant locomotives, and a giant
Steel works.

The second lake lies
At the foot of a hill and is clean
To the point of invisibility. On one side
Is the club where dead Englishmen
Sit down on tigers and play bridge.
Specks of dust drift through their moustached faces.
In the billiard room the table is still
Intact, while the stained kitchen knife
Has appeared in the region's
Folklore.

Natural History

The dawn horse
Fixed on screws
Among painted craters

Looks sideways
Through the glass wall
At the changed wilderness.

The Studio

You hit us across our small clear heads
When our backs were turned
The sun was in our eyes
The sky unclouded

One day you will lie where we do now
And black ants
Like moving particles of light
Will surround you

The blue rose is hidden in the garden
You are writing a poem
Seven cells have been robbed of their spirits
And the wasps know their curse

Yaddo, 1972

Where Will the Next One Come From

The next one will come from the air
It will be an overripe pumpkin
It will be the missing shoe

The next one will climb down
From the tree
When I'm asleep

The next one I will have to sow
For the next one I will have
To walk in the rain

The next one I shall not write
It will rise like bread
It will be the curse coming home

Declines

Come in. It is night.
The wind has risen.
The trees are like dark
Pools of sound.
I must speak with you,
Compare your wings
With my counterfeiting fingers.
The stars

Rock like boats.
Who makes your annual
Itinerary? Who taught you
To invoke the land?
The meridian's friend,
Your frame of clear glass
Guides your flight.
The horizon

Is tense like a bow.
Your calico-coloured wings
Spread and rise
Unhurriedly through the air.
Teach me to weave.

Company Period

Of Zayn-ul-din, 'an artist of Patna',
Little is known except that he painted
Around 1780 a few Indian subjects
For Lady Impey.
Trained in the Mughal workshops,
He adapted himself to the needs
Of the period: English paper and watercolour
Technique. Lady Impey's interest
In native artists was partly 'scientific',
So when she left for home she possessed
A portrait of herself in her Bengal
Drawing room, and a complete set
Of the flora and fauna as well.
Zayn-ul-din's cheetah was in it.
The cheetah is shown in profile. Hind legs
Curved, a triple band on the tail, small
Overlapping spots on the neck. A fresh pug mark
In the bottom left corner, Zayn-ul-din's signature.

On the Death of a Sunday Painter

He smoked a cherrywood pipe, knew all about cannas,
And deplored our lack of a genuine fast bowler.
My uncle called his wife Soft Hands.
Once in 1936 as he sat reading *Ulysses*
In his Holland Hall drawing room, a student walked in.
Years later I read him an essay on D.H. Lawrence
And the Imagists. He listened,
Then spoke of Lord Clive, the travels of Charles Doughty,
'My dear young fellow...'
I followed the mourners on my bicycle
And left early. His friends watched the cremation
From the portico of a nearby house.

After Kabir

I
Another's wife
Is a knife.
Don't touch her limbs.

II
A hungry woman
Is a lamed tigress.
She gobbles you up.

III
Show me the forkless road,
Lead me till there;
Or between two rivers
Make me a hut;
Or engrave your face
On my body's parchment.

IV
This arbour of thorns
Will enclose you,
This dry bush will burn.
A day is three parts sunset, says Kabir.

V

Prince or pauper,
Mendicant or thief,
Once you arrive
You must depart.
One rides to his grave on a horse,
The other trudges behind a cart.

VI

The kings shall go, so will their pretty queens,
The courtiers and the proud ones shall go.
Pundits reciting the *Vedas* shall go,
And go will those who listen to them.
Masochist yogis and bright intellectuals shall go,
Fathers and sons, nights and days shall go.
Thus, says Kabir, only those shall remain
Whose minds are tied to the rocks.

VII

There's enough ink
To fill seven seas,
Enough paper
To cover the hills.
It won't even do
For the first verse, says Kabir.

After Maluk

I

Put the flying mountain
Through a needle's eye,
Grow a mango
Without planting the tree,
Lay bricks and remain homeless,
Create light without the wick,
Fix a nail in the sea,
Tie an elephant to a moth,
Cross the sky on one wing,
Ride a boat on parched land,
And you're his disciple.
See the world
Without leaving your window,
And I'm your friend.
The best magicians, says Maluk, are children.

II

A woman has bitten me:
I've forgotten the colour of her hair,
I've preserved the shape of her teeth.
A remedy like this, says Maluk,
Is worth a kingdom.

III

Keep your room empty
And your sheet of paper clean.
There's no greater discipline, says Maluk.

IV

It's a hundred years old,
It has neither entry nor exit,
It's a burnt stick of wood.
My father's house, says Maluk, is an answer
To which I've lost the riddle.

V

Face west, take vows,
Wear caps, count beads,
And he's indifferent;
Stay at home,
Leave the door open,
And he'll come visiting.
Nobody's listening to Maluk any more.

VI

Look at me:
Without a brother, without kinsmen,
Without a tribe.
Without a friend who'd give me a night's shelter.
Without gold and silver bars hidden under the floor.
Without a penny in my purse.
Without a farm; without even a vegetable patch.
Without a trade.
Where's the moneylender I could borrow from?
An occasional word, says Maluk, is all I need.

VII

If it's gold you'll hide it from your son.
If it's tinsel you'll tell the whole countryside.
If you hear any chanting, says Maluk,
Pull out your mattress and go to sleep.

from Middle Earth

(1984)

Classification

Are trees vertebrate? Spikenards are.
Some bones soft as pistils
Are trampled on by wood-ants.
I was crushed by the bone I sat on.
Clever bone, you're one of these:
I returned from a voyage
With a bone in my mouth,
Under a glass bell it spread wings
And dropped two talons;
The white bone is the queen bone;
The more complex bones have a mind
And die of seizure.
They're buried by headless poppets.

1972

The Exquisite Corpse

Smoke makes faces, ladders burn
Children who don't love me
Are lifted by hyenas

Once a year I inventory my cellar
The old woman's alone in her shoe
Georgie Porgie's a pimply beau

A cluster of bamboo walking sticks
Force open my father's chest
The goat is dead, long live the baa

1972

Let's Face It

The lower classes, my dear, are indestructible.
Buff sunsets gather dust in mustard fields
And if the rains fail this hat tree will die.

1975

House by the Mill

A woman addresses the nation;
    What big ears she has.
The fabulous Red Riding Hoods
    In gladed wood
Burn flare-ups, but freedom's too prudent
    To risk its skin.
O house by the mill we're trapped in.

26 June 1975*

*The day Prime Minister Indira Gandhi declared the Emergency.

Bhojpuri Descant
(After Ghagha)

I
Piss after dinner,
Sleep on your left side:
You'll never be sick.

II
If landlords are saints,
Pestles are bowstrings.

III
Witty landlords,
Wheezy thieves:
Lynch them.

IV
A servant who knows
The secrets of the house,
A pretty wife,
Spetched clothes,
A wicked king:
They need careful handling.

V
A shoe that pinches,
A sharp-tongued wife,
The first-born a daughter,

An unproductive farm,
An idiot brother:
They cause endless grief.

VI
A brown she-elephant,
A bald wife,
Rain in winter:
Signs of luck.

VII
Three oxen, two wives:
Trouble's at your doorstep.

VIII
A spendthrift son,
A cross-eyed buffalo,
A moody ox:
Get rid of them at once.

IX
An ox with six teeth
Will change hands quickly,
An ox with seven
Will butt its owner,
An ox with nine
Will run in nine directions
And won't spare even the family priest.

X
To inspect the teeth
Of a skewbald ox
Is a waste of time.

XI
A thin-tailed ox
With a swamp deer's piss
Brings prosperity.

XII
A blue-flanked ox
With purple horns
Can't go wrong.

XIII
One plough is death,
Two's survival,
Three's good business,
Four's a kingdom.

XIV
A wise farmer does his own tilling,
The one less wise walks beside his team,
But the farmer who goes looking for tillmen
Loses his seeds.

XV
A small ploughshare
Tickles the field.

XVI
A kite's screech from atop a ruin:
Sign of rain.

XVII
A chameleon
Scrambles up a tree
Tail first:
Expect a flood.

XVIII
Clouds throughout the day,
A clear sky at night:
Famine.

XIX
The clouds from the west are misers.

Telegram

for A.J.

The wick sputters and this
Chirp is from the hopper
In my mind. The floor is
Cold. I dip my toes in
It. Someone pushes me
From behind and my whoo-
Pee plunges into the
Deep end's icy water.
He's running towards the
Bottle-green shore, waving
His arms, his ship anchored
In his mind's inlet, his
Cabined keyboard ablaze.

The Cotton Tree

I
A badminton-net away
    From each
Other and bang
    In front of
A half-dilapidated
    One-
Storey forties house,
    Two
Great Indian cotton trees.
    Nothing is
Alive in this
    Abstract
Distance from X
    To Y
Except their brittle
    Shade.
Moth-like sun-patches
    Alight
On each hurrying
    Arm, nape,
And nose-tip,
    Even as shadows,
Stepping straight out of
    Lime-washed
Walls, chase them
    Away.
A lingering nip
    In the
Air; March eighty-
    Two;
Summer's first lap.

II
A boy walking
    Ahead of
Us, carrying a
    Milk pail in
One hand, an eyeless
    Taxidermied
Calf in the other,
    Divides his
Attention between kites
    Fighting
In the sky and the pair of
    Taw-eyed
Buffaloes under his
    Charge. From 37
Paternoster Row, James
    Duncan
Published in MDCCCXXX
    A thirty-volume
Description of someone's
    Travels
Round the globe. Silverfish
    Have made
A meal of it, eating away
    The kerns,
Leaving the shanks
    Of letters alone.
I sometimes wonder
    If all
The leaves that ever fell
    Are not
Inside this page.

III
They did not fall
    But drifted
Upwards through the
    Valved
Air. Overnight the trees
    Stood
Upside down, their
    Branches
Lit with comets'
    Misty
Tails. On land,
    The wind
Smelt of hot
    Cross buns.
Our route didn't change,
    Though sometimes
When a dust storm blew
    We covered
Just half the distance.
    Single crows
Darted across a flat
    Sky
Towards unfallen nests.
    The trees
Were a
    Settlement.
They're now pieces
    Of uncased
Machinery, left
    On a
Watchmaker's table.

The Roys

We've rented a flat in Ghosh Buildings, Albert Road,
And the Roys live across the street. Mr Roy,
General Merchant, dresses in white
Drill trousers, long-sleeved cotton shirts,
And looks like a friendly duck.
His three sons are in school with me. The eldest,
Ganesh, has a gleaming forehead,
A shelled-egg complexion, a small
Equilateral mouth. He belongs to a mystical
Group of philatelists. Together with Shaporjee,
The tallow-white Parsi next door, and Roger Dutt,
The school's aromatic geography teacher, he goes up
In an air balloon and, on the leeward
Side of a Stanley Gibbons catalogue, comes down
Near a turret in Helvetia or Magyar,
Stamp-sized snowflake-like countries
Whose names dissolve like jujubes on my tongue.
We play French cricket, seven tiles, I spy, and Injun.
Our tomahawks are butter-knives, our crow
Feathers are real, and riding out from behind
Plaza Talkies we ambush the cowboys of Civil Lines.
Ganesh does not join our games. The future,
He seems to say, is not a doodle on the back
Of an envelope but a scarp to be climbed
Alone. He attends a WUS* meeting in Stockholm
And opens a restaurant in the heart of town.
I go there in early youth for Jamaican coffee,
In early middle age to use its toilet.
From behind the counter he extends his hand.

*World University Service.

'How's the English Department?' he asks. 'How's
Rajamani? Is Mishra a professor now? Is that true?
What are things coming to.' As I listen to him
My piss travels down the left trouser leg
Into my sock, and then my restless son drags me
Towards a shoe store and buys his first pair of
Naughty Boys. Seen from the road,
Mr Roy's shop is a P&O boat anchored in midstream.
Inside, it's an abandoned coal pit. A film
Of darkness wraps the merchandise; a section of the far
Wall conceals the mouth of a cave, leading
To an underground spring; the air, dry and silvery
At the entrance, is moist and sea-green, furry
To the touch; the display cases, embedded
In the floor, are stuffed with a galleon's treasure;
Finned toffees peer at customers through glass jars.
Every afternoon Mr Roy goes home for his
Siesta and his second son, Ramesh, still wearing
A crumpled school uniform, takes over the town's
Flagship. At three p.m. the roads melt, becoming
Impassable, as cloth-backed chiks
Protect shopfronts against heatstroke.
For the next two hours the sun, stationed above
A traffic island, lays siege to the town, and the only
Movement is of leaves falling so slowly
That midway through their descent their colours
Change. The two waxen shop assistants
Melt in their sticks, Ramesh sits beside
The cash box with an open sesame
Look in his eye, and I have the place
All to myself. Looking around,
I can make out, in the small light coming in
From outside, bottles of ketchup, flying cigarillos,

Death-feigning penknives, tooth powders, inexpensive
Dragon china dinner sets, sapphire-blue packets
Of detergent, wooden trays holding skeins
Of thread, jade-coloured boxes of hosiery, rolled-gold
Trinkets, mouth-watering dark-tan shoe polish, creams,
And hula hoops. Driven by two ceiling fans,
The freighter moves. Land drops from sight.
Though the binoculars are trained on the earth's dip,
The eye is monopolized by afterimages of land:
I hold a negative against the light,
And now I'm received into the negative I'm holding.
At five p.m. the spell is broken. The sun
Calls it a day and goes down, Mr Roy comes
To clear away the jungle that has grown around his shop,
And I slip away with a packet of razor blades.
Where stealing's easy, hiding stolen goods is tough.
A pink stamp issued on Queen Elizabeth's coronation
Cannot be traced to a cigarette tin buried among
Clothes, but what do I do with a whole album
That has the owner's name rubber stamped
All over it? To six-year-old Suresh I give lessons
In the pleasures of thieving.
For each first-day cover he brings, I press
My View-Master against his face
And let him look through it once. Then one day, while
Having lunch, I see a policeman framed in the door.
The food in my mouth hardens into a lump
Of plaster of Paris. Afterwards, I lose my voice
And so does everyone around me. Believe me when I say
That nothing's more sad than a tropical evening,
When auctioneers buy dead advocates' libraries
And there's all the time in the world and nowhere to go.
Their cousin, Anil, takes out his autograph book.

'Just in case,' he says, 'you become famous.'
He has said this to every boy in school.
'Do you think,' he asks, 'I can get Peeks's
Grandfather's autograph?' Peeks's grandfather is a retired
Chief justice and gets his pension in sterling.
Anil takes a hard look at a marble
In the hollow of his palm
But can't make out if it's an oblong. His sister,
The same age as us but more hairy,
To whom strange things happen, sits
On the verandah, absorbed in our game.
Through broken tiles in the roof
Sunbeams let themselves down and she screams
Before they strike her. She turns
Into a black beetle and crawls on my skin. Charlie Hyde,
Nicknamed Bony Arse, is the only other person
To so affect me. We go our separate ways and sometimes
We cross Albert Road together or meet outside
A chemist's. Anil has a tabletop head, a broad forehead,
And bulging brown eyes. He sets himself up
As a dealer in office equipment
And then as a distributor for Number Ten cigarettes.
He fails at both jobs and is given shock therapy.

New Golden

The mirror in front
    Of me reflects the mirror
Behind me. Lightly
    Bearded, thirtyish,
Standing between them,
    A rough-looking
Man takes off his
    Coffee-brown shirt
And holds his right
    Arm above his head
For Lallu
    Of New Golden
Hairdressers
    To approach it,
Which he, stropped
    Cut-throat in hand, does
From the side.
    Then he shaves
The left pit.
    'Twice Sardar
Squeezed the tiger*
    And it jammed
Both times.
    Close, wasn't it?'

*Trigger

'The World's a Printing-House'

There's a mountain in my mind,
    I must be true to it.
        There's a mountain in
            My mind and I
                Must read it
                    Line by
                        Line

Or it will disappear. Cone
    Of light or natal space,
        Call it what you will,
            I must be true
                To it. Clouds
                    Sweep its
                      Base,

Terraces cut into its
    Summit, windows into
        Its slopes, through which pours
            The mountain side:
                The mountain
                    In my
                      Mind,

Grazing on itself, and its
    Own reflection. Inversed
        Peak, clapperless Great
            Tom, some unfelt
                Entirely
                  Visioned
                    Thing,

Fading across the rent veil.
Like a compositor's
Radiant font, in my
Mind a mountain;
I must be
True to
It.

Location

Close to midnight, the honk
    Honk of a speeding
Jeep rattles the message
    Sent over a cyclist's
Two-band; near the loco
    Shed, dogs bait an idling
Diesel, then they regroup
    And bark again when
The goods has passed; at
    The bottom of page 276 of
Studies in medieval perspective,
    Robertson writes, 'No one
Thought in terms of
    Psychology in the fourteenth
Century any more than he
    Thought in terms of
Differential calculus.'
    Couldn't agree, couldn't
Disagree with the sentence
    And stopped reading.
In my hands I held this poem.

Disiecti Membra Poetae

The east wind and
    A lizard rampant
Spell rain;
    Pencils
Stab dictionaries
    In the dark;
Frigate-birds
    Put rings
Round the moon;
    The smell
Of ink and
    The shape of
Wyoming;
    Colours like
Burma green,
    Words like
'Slough'; off-rhymes,
    Translations,
Dead metaphors,
    Things:
The flywheels and
    Sprockets,
The gristle
    Of poems,
Tossed in sleep's
    Fountain,
Garnered in nests,
    Recalled
In holograph,
    At places

Smudged, late for
   Assemblage.

Uncollected Poems

1985–1995

Annual

Begin, begin, the year will end,
    Time add a new ring to its stem,
And the cage of the unlived mind
    Resound with the passing bell.

Retired men sit on culverts,
    There's no shade in young trees,
Sparrows hop to the edge
    And whirr off balconies.

The tower has unequal steps,
    How many is hard to tell.
Quicker a fall to the bottom
    Of the dark stairwell.

The Secondhand Trade

The tradesman looks around.
    The merchandise on sale
Threadbare and stained,
    Is stacked on the day's
Counter. Above it, on walls,
    The discount sign.
The air is dry. The till
    Makes an empty sound.

Sometimes the doorbell
    Rings. The wrong doorbell.
Completely grey, his life
    Past change, he sometimes
Changes the display, or bent
    Over a long mango wood
Table, repairs a buttonhole
    Or buckle.

Bad for Verse

Middle age is bad for verse,
Specially for a surrealist.
A loss of vision is a loss of words.

What went wrong? He doesn't know.
The morning light still falls on leaves.
The man he was died years ago.

Now, sitting in an easy chair,
He stares at the blank wall in front,
Shading the eyes to cut the glare.

In Swich Licour

More than green and
    Less then yellow,
A flame of sound
    With veins of ink,
In the lamp's light,
    In morocco,
I want to see
    The leaf outside.

Bring the vessel
    And my eyesight,
Set the bottled
    Spirits loose.
Shut the window,
    Draw down the blinds,
I want to see
    The leaf outside.

Three Songs

I

The cat-faced hyena
    In the laughing grass
Seems in no hurry
    To stalk his prey.
A newborn isn't known
    To walk away.

II

I found a word
    Abstract and rare,
As tall as once
    And twice as fair.

Its hands were cold,
    Its feet were bare,
It had a rope
    Around the neck.

I brought it down
    And wiped its face;
I set it free
    And took its place.

III
Things that make us
    Melt like ice,
Things that burn us
    Soothe the eyes.

Things that touch us
    Never do,
Things that stop us
    Take us through.

Crooked Pictures

Pushing open a door, before I can reach for the switch,
Someone inside turns on the light.

I see thick stone walls hung with crooked pictures;
A teapoy, its leg broken, slumped in a corner;
A rolled up carpet, too old to show the good days it's seen;
A pair of brogues, with curled tongues.
There's a man standing near the fireplace. It's my father,
Who, dead twelve years, is still soft spoken,
Who speaks in the things he's left behind,
Who, living, dispossessed himself of his one life.

The Fatal Thread

Tomorrow the drongo
    Will sit on the pole,
The bell ring or someone yell.

Tomorrow the squirrel
    Will cross the yard,
The mongoose test the snake.

Tomorrow the sun
    Will not rise nor set,
Nor time extend the fatal thread.

Approaching My Fortieth Year

Tuning the radio, what do I hear?
There are red giants and white dwarfs.
New stars born every minute,
The old ones cooling off.

Astronomer in the mountain,
Look again with the naked eye.
Is there a second message
For us from the sky?

The sun is far from finished,
But who will receive its light?
The earth's without cover
And asteroids roam the night.

Lines Written in a Young Lady's Album

It cannot be that fathering men
    Won't love again, will turn
Their backs for good on tall windows
    Below which as beardless boys they stood,
The skinny lovers of bosomy girls.
    Why can't we be like this always?
They'll say in a voice split down
    The middle. They've said it once before,
The wind slipping in
    Through cracks in the door.

The Transfiguring Places

(1998)

Approaching Fifty

Sometimes,
In unwiped bathroom mirrors,
He sees all three faces
Looking at him:

His own,
The grey-haired man's
Whose life policy has matured,
And the mocking youth's
Who paid the first premium.

Dry Farming

What do I measure, what do I sing?
    Sing the heart's seizure, the fall
Of a king, so what if it's
    Been sung before. So has the handicapped
Man waiting for the traffic to thin, so has
    The close at hand, the ode
To a safety pin. Or sing
    The spread virus, the song everyone
Knows, ripped city buses and house full
    Matinée shows. But if song
Dies in the tongue and all known methods
    Fail, remember books, the other
Land, the double of the world
    Outside, and to the terror
Of the unspoilt sheet
    Bring the joy of *A Reader's Guide*.

Borges

Before the Ganges flows into the night,
    Before the knife rusts, the dream lose
Its crescent shape, before the tiger runs
    For cover in your pages, Borges, I must
Write the poem. Insomnia brings lucidity,
    And a borrowed voice sets the true one
Free: lead me who am no more than De Quincey's
    Malay, a speechless shadow in a world
Of sound, to the labyrinth of the earthly
    Library, perfect me in your work.

Inscription

Last night a line appeared,
Unbidden, unsigned:
It had eight memorable
Syllables. I'll keep you,

I said, falling asleep.
It's gone now,
And I write this to requite it,
And to mark its passage.

Memoranda

The milk's delivered at six o'clock.
Try nature cure for writer's block.

Travel north in a southbound train,
And cross the desert on the wheels of rain.

Unload the boats anchored in the bay.
Deepen the channel, dredge out the clay.

Once the hum stops there's nothing you can do.
Your best lines those that didn't come through.

Tongue-tied at times, at times colour-blind,
Go fishing then. There's nothing wrong with your mind.

View the passing show with an inward eye.
The average man is only five foot high.

Art is long, who doesn't know that.
Keep pedalling, my friend, though the tyre's flat.

If not this the next mile of verses
Could be the *annus mirabilis.*

At Seasons

In the close heat of summer
　　An Iowa winter besets me –
An apartment in The Mayflower,
　　My happy wife learning pottery.

In winter, the wet monsoon –
　　Frog songs, low rumbling clouds,
Insects crawling on the arm,
　　A heron shooting off its mouth.

On loony nights,
　　Across the sealed window,
Hot winds chase
　　Midwestern snow.

The Storm

There was little to tell it from
The other places we passed, Deoband,
Khatauli, the peasant towns of western
Uttar Pradesh. The June day was windless,
The sky a boiling white. The bus had made
An unscheduled halt. The driver was talking
With a garage hand. We waited for him
To start and passed the time looking at
The hoardings on rooftops, the women
Standing in littered doorways with children
At their hips, the men, unshaven,
Sitting beside parked trucks, drinking tea.
Two blasts of the horn sounded and those
Who'd got down to stretch their legs
Hurried back. As the bus picked up speed,
I saw it quivering in the heat-haze, a place
Whose name I hadn't known nor asked,
Which I sometimes think was Shiraz, or a firth
In the North Sea from where the skalds set out.
The next day there was a storm,
And the hail melted as fast as it fell.

Ramapithecus and I

The young swamp he came to
Six million years ago,
His unfazed mother beside him,
His father recently dead,

Is the wall map's mixed forest,
A dotted power line along its edge,
And the window's low, clouded hills,
Dolomite and fossil rich.

Making his home
Where his implements took him,
He waited for the rains to break.
Cutting my finger, it's his blood I taste.

Summer Notes

I
Mother in front, with shopping bag
    And umbrella; I in the middle;
Behind me a bespectacled
    Grandfatherly hodman carrying
A light load of bricks. The air
    Was clear as a bell that morning.
Back at my desk, night's events –
    Moon, jackfruit tree, homing swallow –
Overtaking the window, hourglass sand
    The hour, I fell asleep. Our days
Filled with insubstantial things,
    We dream to make up for lost time.

II
Evening, a book in my hand,
    Feet crossed on a plank of light
Slanting through the door,
    In the northern sky a cloud
About the size of Ireland looks down.

One by one lines darken
    On the unread page and early stars
Appear to take sides: going in,
    A phrase singing in my head,
A light rain of rhythms surrounds me.

III

Empty lorries pass us and a bored
    Holiday-maker waves from a bus.
Turning into a sidestreet we're enclosed
    In an ex-brigadier's garden,
Where behind tall hedges and under
    A parrotless sky dwarf mango trees
Carry on all fours full grown
    Fruit. Walking back past inconspicuous
Grocers' shops, our own lives
    Seeming blessed with retirement, a new
Bustle in the evening air: the sight
    Of common birds in exuberant flight.

IV

There's a world so they may seek advantage.
    Tumours, lyings-in, disorders of the skin,
Jobs and killings: the conversation
    Of the unfailably married gathered round
A tea wagon. A deaf-mute, a servant's daughter,
    Hops on the grass where a mongrel
Yawns; parked cars inch forward
    In receding light. 'How did the shaddock tree die?'
I ask. A rockery where faded zinnias grow
    Forces its trunk and crumbly leaves
Hang at long intervals from
    Mortified branches; the ivy
That lashed it from base to crown sinking
    Petioles into the bark, rises in victorious tiers
On an adjoining wall. 'The last fruit
    Was its sweetest,' someone says at the gate
As we leave our hosts, the hooded ivy, the poisoned
    Quarry, the animal kingdom of plants.

Old Survey Road

Where the land slopes
Toward the riverbed's
No man's land,
At the compound's edge,
Is a single tree,

Which is three trees
Grown from one sapling,
Or three saplings
Grown into one tree,
Mango, litchi, and peach

Ripening on its branches.
No botany textbook
Or illustrated dictionary
Gives its picture,
But in the record-breaking

Temperature of June,
The month of forest fires,
The green of parakeets
Flares in its foliage
And thieving children

Scrimmage in its shade.
To me their bruised knees
Recall similar injuries,
Some yet to heal,
Others become rings.

The Inheritance

I
They were here
    Last night, outlaws,
Woodmen, visitors who came
    Nine years after
You died.

My mouth tasted
    Of sand. They
Sipped lemonade; stripped
    A family tree
Of foliage.

She took
    The silver, and he
The jade. I'll make,
    As I've this, a nest
In emptiness.

II
As others before you, you came here
    To die under trees
That as a boy you'd climbed. Where

The litchi stood, east of the tennis court,
    Is now a ditch, some
Kind man has covered with wild rose.

III
You left me sunset, the light
Of the polestar; to save me from summer
You left me the north, a strip of land
In that sad direction

To which I'm always returning. Among
Such articles I inherit, the gift
I brought you, a pair of socks, one size
Too big, for that is how fathers

Appear to sons, grown old themselves
In rented houses far from home.
I look at your hiding places again:
A shaving mirror; an aunt's profile.

IV
These rooms open
    Memory's stitches:
Your hand on my shoulder;
    The kiss on departure;
The letters, even the last,
    That gave nothing away.

Then the valley
    Seen from afar,
In a window's quiet,
    In a map on the wall,
Birds coming to
    Divided gardens.

The House

In the middle
Of a forest,
A house of stone.

Bats in the rafters,
Bat dung on the floor,
And hanging from a nail

A dentist's coat
Smelling pleasantly
Of chloroform.

Mud on his sandals
And smoke in his eyes,
On a railway platform

I saw him last,
Who passes before me
In the cheval-glass.

Locking Up
for I. Allan Sealy

Was that a barbet I heard
In the jujube tree,
Or walking sticks rattling
In an empty cupboard?
Are questions I ask
All summer long.
Then when vacation ends,
We pack our bags,
Lock up the place,
And return to the plains.

Not everything the ears hear
Can the tongue repeat: family lore,
The pied myna's call,
The blathering
Of a loose-tongued door,
The secrets that crawl
Out of dead servants' mouths.
My own snaps shut,
And I fall asleep listening
To the clickety-clack of the train.

It's taking me back
To the house I've just locked.
It is winter.
I'm sitting in a wheelchair,
A rug wrapped round the knees,
Watching postmen go past the front gate
With nothing for me,

The afternoons
Getting longer each year,
And the light not dimming.

The Photograph
New Delhi, 1958

Amolak Ram Mehta and
Shanti Devi are flanked by
Their daughters and
A daughter-in-law;

Behind them,
In dark suits that'll
Never fade, the husbands
Stand shoulder to shoulder;

The grandchildren
Sit on the ground,
In front of their mothers.
At a distance of some ten feet,

Looking like a piece of ordnance,
Is the camera.
Mr Mahatta, the photographer,
Lowers the black cloth and

Stepping forward, clicks.
Amolak Ram Mehta is dead,
So are the sons-in-law,
And his adoring children

Have carried the photograph
To Kalamazoo and Vancouver.
One's remained in my mother's room.
She's had it for years

Above her bed
And never taken it down.
The spiders that live in it
Are of a golden colour.

The Fracture

Your mother is seventy.
One day she slips
And breaks her wrist.

You are not there
When this happens.
You are in Islington.

It is six weeks
Before you see her.
You take her to the doctor.

He asks her to open
And close her palm,
And she does as she is told.

He explains
Barton's fracture
To you

And holds a X-ray
Against the light.
You don't understand a thing

But nod all the same
And ask if they do
Hip replacement in Dehra Dun.

I'm doing one this afternoon,
He says,
Filling another column

In her insurance form.
Your mother asks
If she should take more calcium.

My father, she says,
Sucked on bones
To make his own more strong

And lived to be ninety.
In two days
You have a train to catch

And are careful
About reaching her home
Safely.

Before leaving,
You advise her to be
More active

And to take long walks.

I Cannot Live Here All My Life

I cannot live here all my life.
The hour is set and streets explode.
A quiet man pulls out a knife.

They ride in peace who're born in strife,
The by-blows of the Golden Horde.
I cannot live here all my life.

Quick as death, the boys arrive.
Three go in, two watch the road.
A quiet man pulls out a knife.

It's like being buried alive.
Under the rubble lies one who said,
I cannot live here all my life.

As muscles waste and scars revive,
In the mind's pit left unexplored,
A quiet man pulls out a knife.

Eyewitnesses go blind, survive
The blown mouth. A mouth is closed.
I cannot live here all my life.
A quiet man pulls out a knife.

Scenes from a Revolving Chair

I
Day after day, the outlook unchanged,
The long walk through elephant grass
In search of common speech. Sometimes
The nights are spent
In the middle of a borderless page,
And sometimes, unbroken clouds
Of late August darkening the frontier,
A wind rises in the octave branches.

II
The book lies open on two-voiced
Summer: the hawk-cuckoo's
Grey and white lines through hazeless
Air; overleaf, illuminated,
The copper-pod's long measures.
Standing like a bronze statue
In a public square, the city
Reads from the seasons.

III
After a heatwave and a night of storms
Have covered porcelain and rosewood
With a sheet woven with the threads
Of dust and rain,
A blue morning revives outside,
Offering to eyes what eyes cannot
Accept, unless a hand retouch
The unknowable picture.

IV

Without lifting their wings
The prey-birds climb
And fill the sky's dyed ground,
Throwing quilled shadows
Even as they move
Away from the eddying
River of consonants, the vowels that drown
Before leaden boats can reach them.

V

The moist-browed houses bury their dead
In unmarked valleys: the fanlight-eye
On which light does not fall,
The coping on which hard rain,
The bureau that will not be injured
By letters again. Steadily, for ever
Steadily, a sixty-year-old man
Blazes against a trembling wall.

Dream-Figures in Sunlight

*Why buy Bret Harte, I asked, when I was prepared
to supply home-grown fiction on the hoof?*
     —Rudyard Kipling, *Something of Myself*

I wake up in the city where Kipling lived,
Fell in love and wrote plain tales,
Where Hsiuan-tsang in the seventh century
Saw mortal pilgrims making death leaps

From an undying tree. The rampart stands,
The Ganges flows below, and nothing changes
In a hinterland whose dead-end streets
Have seldom known raiders. A hundred, a thousand

Years from now, may the sap-filled bough
Still print its shadow on running water,
And a dusty March wind blow its leaves
Towards a page of Kipling, a home-grown page.

Domicile

For the slashed cheek
And puckered knee
And unkept vow,

But as much for
The trips not made
To places of interest –

Like the Stone Age site
A bus ride away
In Mirzapur District –

Accept in recompense
This cone of light
In whose spell I sit,

A mechanical pencil
Gripped in my hand,
Like a microlith.

Last View from Church Lane

From rented rooms
The view of a tower
That broadcast rock pigeons
From the belfry when the hour

Struck, till one day
The irreparable chime-barrel
Clogged with droppings
And a wide crack appeared

Between minute and minute-hand.
We've changed too. My voice
Has grown blustery; yours
Is still as a moth's wings.

The Vase That Is Marriage

The vase is the painted figure
Of a vase, like a postcard-size print
Of, say, a still life with pawpaw.

The tablecloth is brown,
As in maps a mountain range is brown,
But the Java Sea is green, in which the vase,

Dragging its anchor, is a sailing junk.
The tablecloth is a hank of yarn,
Which doesn't make the vase potter's clay.

It never was that anyway.
When did he last, seeing the vase as a vase,
Put some flowers in, or not lack the desire?

To an Unborn Daughter

If writing a poem could bring you
Into existence, I'd write one now,
Filling the stanzas with more
Skin and tissue than a body needs,
Filling the lines with speech.
I'd even give you your mother's

Close-bitten nails and light-brown eyes,
For I think she had them. I saw her
Only once, through a train window,
In a yellow field. She was wearing
A pale-coloured dress. It was cold.
I think she wanted to say something.

Chekhov Retold

No Yalta this, no lilac-hued sea,
Nor the time mid-autumn, but a district town
Of cobwebs and visitants, a night's journey

From the nearest coast. The March day
Unseasonably hot and the quarter hour,
By a one-armed clock, struck in a bee-hived tower.

From the west a sirocco-like wind blowing,
Dragging a boy's kite, torn on one side,
To the meagre canopy of a myrobalan tree,

Buffalo cows mooing under it. Further
Up the road, in a margosa's leafless shade,
Unaware of the wide-eyed passers-by,

A man and a younger woman, his daughter's age,
Meet like thieves and a lap dog barks.
Where but in fiction are the lives they lead?

The Transfiguring Places

They teach you how to survive in the wild,
How stalk a quarry, what roots to eat,
Outdoor skills of no use in the street,
Where in sola hat of branching horns you chase

In grass and air the scent marks not there.
It's in the mind, the transfiguring
Trysting places (banks, grocery stores) and
The trees you walk under, escaping,

Their leaves burning like light bulbs in the day
And a wind, long-toed, jostling you back
To the rear of a queue or the edge
Of a street, leaving you stamping the ground

With your feet and shaking your hatted head.
Wise up, I say, there's no running away
But taking the crushed counterfoil or receipt
In your pocket in your composite stride.

The Reading Room

In a latitude where the nights
Are short and starless
Sitting on either side of a table
We expertly pitch our tent at end of day
Unable to see you in the failing light
I construct your mind from what you have to say

You tell me about a butterfly's wood-brown wings
The birdsong at five a.m.
That woke you like an alarm
The desires of a mongrel bitch
Who litters in the cool of your verandah
A poem by Carlos Drummond de Andrade that begins
'Carlos, keep calm, love/is what you're seeing now'

You tell me about servants who are voyeurs
Fathers who are forgiving
Music masters and second lieutenants
You've driven crazy
An acquaintance who on second meeting
Confided her latest affair
You tell me about the wild times in Kalimpong

You tell me about hillsides and siblings
Pine cones and star signs
Law suits and pets
You tell me you're a schoolgirl again
Discovering afresh in a candy-striped dress
The cloven leaf and the parts of a flower
You tell me how clever you are

As the kettle hisses
And you keep talking
My stretched hand touching
The raised lines of your skin
I want to tell you it's nothing you say
But the singing voice you say it in

Tailor-Bird

Bring it to me, I'll
    Turn your life,
The tailor-bird said.
    I was listening.

Reading the sports page
    One Thursday morning,
I saw her darting out
    Of a flowering tree.

Heading the wrong way,
    She kept coming
Towards me, stolen thread
    Held in her beak,

To tack on my jacket
    A tailor-bird's wings.
(I found you in the dust,
    She would say.)

The door still ajar,
    And she calling out,
The terrazzo floor
    Dropping below me,

I sailed in fields
    Where gale-winds blew
But each leaf
    Was still, as if

On a windless day.
    Then evening fell,
The living room's
    Colours changed,

The gates
    Of the mausoleum
Closed for the night,
    And small birds

With their love-cries
    Filled a flowering tree.
Looking up
    From the sports page

I heard
    A tailor-bird say,
Bring it to me,
    I'll turn your life.

Nautical 1

Those jetty lights are wax candles
    Flickering over bald cabbages.
At makeshift stalls behind
    The Accountant General's office,
Grey-stubbled, fecund, homebound clerks –
    Their last-born the same age
As their first grandchild –
    Haggle for perishables.
Their frenzied voices roll and heave
    As she comes into view, vanishes,
Reappears, weighed down by stout canvas
    Shopping bags, and squeezing
The car keys in her hand.
    As she comes alongside,
And for what seems a long time,
    Out of the corner of her eye
Watches me watching her buy
    Cucumbers and spring onions.

Nautical 2

Early travellers to upland towns
And the Coromandel coast, whose feet
Trod the ground but walked on the sea,
Have left accounts of mermaid sightings.

I sighted one as I ran across a street
On an errand. The traffic light was green,
And cars, their headlamps dipped, braked or swerved.
I bought a loaf and took the same route home.

The return felt shorter, the luminous ports
Seen in reverse order. The sky was black,
As before a storm, as I came ashore,
Scaly-thighed and with weed-hung arms.

From a Neoteric Codex

Better, by far, the black economy
Of night. By the stars short changed,
To have leaped over a magistrate's gate
At dawn and shoeless fled across
The dung-pits of Rome, than stood
Twitchingly at noon in comical
Disguise and as the cuckoo clocks chimed
At one blow passed from stunned old age
To erect youth and back, only worse,
The insides upside down and hanging out.
Fish, coming up to the aquarium wall,
Glued their noses to it and watched,
As they did on the day, since erased, when,
A Hamadryad in spring, recumbent
On a couch, you said *Give me poison.*
I wish I had. And yet you won't
Walk out of history just like that,
Unidentified, uncelebrated, and unspat.
One cuts one's losses the best one can,
No Catullus to your Lesbia though I am.

Cedars

In the mountains
No disguise helps.
No beret, camouflage jacket,
And wire-rimmed specs,
No checking into hotels
Under a false name even.

The road narrows,
Becomes steep;
You go past the clock tower,
The silversmiths' shops,
And two cows grazing,
And come upon snow peaks
Glittering like trophies
In the sun.

Nothing prepares you for that,
Or for the hill woman
You stop on the way
To ask about the trees.
She has thick ankles
And a slow walk,
And says they're cedars.

Trouvaille

Too numerous to be hidden safely in books,
The letters keep falling out, the early ones
Unsigned, the latest full of old accusations.
Picking one up I read along the fold,
What makes you say all this is make-believe?

Your round, legible hand, mainly, but also
The earth's shape, the exactness of distances,
The coldness of ice, the happiness of others,
The eight parts of the day, the sight of hills.
Things must remain as they are, and I am changed.

Beggarhood

Loping along back roads,
Or sitting on his verandah
In a deck chair,
Or waiting outside phone booths,
Invisible to none
But himself, he's
The man with 6/6 vision.

It is November
And he sees March,
The jacaranda putting forth
An affluence of mauve blossoms.
To see it in November, though,
Is the bronze coin he seeks –
Small, countable, and legal tender.

The Cartographer

He could draw
Anything once:
Peninsulas;
Archipelagoes;
Grassless, unsettled,
Jagged-edged islands;
Landlocked countries
Of cold latitudes,
Exposed like bricks
When empires fell.
Times and places
Close to the self-applauding heart.

Not any more.
Now he draws less,
And such features only
As memory in receding shows:
Pit-heads
And coal-veins;
Tributaries that fall short of rivers
That fall short of the sea;
The dots of broken
Cease-fire lines;
The yellows and reds
Of internal boundaries.

New Poems

A Hindu Panegyrist Remembers Sultan Mahmud
Ghazna, 1030

The wasting disease was bad enough,
Then he started losing his mind.
Visiting the treasury the week he died,
His jewels on display, he broke down
And wept like a child. Newcomers
Won't believe it, but Ghazna used to be
A miserable little place, known only for
The sweetness of its melons, before he
Changed its face, gave it a skyline
To match Baghdad's. He also changed our lives.
Each year before the onset of winter
He'd set off on his Indian campaign,
And four months later, when he returned
In the spring, the camel trains carrying
The spoils of war took a day and a night
To go past my door. We sang his praises,
He didn't stint on the reward; gold mostly,
But sometimes a string of pearls
Or a silk robe, like the one I'm wearing.

For a Slave King 1
Ghur, 1167

'In reciting the Qur'an,
In dispatching a lance,
He's second to none.
To the imam who put him
Through the fire of learning
He was like a son,'
Said the Nishapur merchant
To Muhammad Ghuri.

Ghuri had heard before
Of Aibak's diverse talents,
But never met him.
He was of uncomely appearance
And had a deformed limb.
He was about seventeen years old.
He had a beardless chin.

What passed through Ghuri's mind
As he made the purchase,
Or what passed through the merchant's
As he rose to leave,
A sack of dirhems by his side,
We don't know.
Perhaps Ghuri foresaw
That the slave he was buying

Would be a slave-king
And didn't mind the high price;
Perhaps the merchant
Was already figuring out
The next deal he'd strike.

For a Slave King 2
Delhi, 1211

Histories may not remember him.
His reign, in which he lost
The provinces his father had won,
Barely lasted a year.

Long enough, though,
To strike a copper coin,
Bearing on the obverse the legend,
'The victorious Aram Shah, the Sultan'.

Mirza Ghalib in Old Age
Delhi, 1868

His eyesight failed him,
But in his soldier's hands,
Still held like a sword,
Was the mirror of couplets.

By every post came
Friends' verses to correct,
But his rosary chain
Was a string of debts.

Our Generation

As others go their ways
we came ours
in sixties Bombay
and stuck together
through thick and thin.
The times evened out.

The one who died
was the reviving sort
and soon revived.

Would the same fate
await us three –
Adil, and Gieve, and me –
the ones who survive.

Bharati Bhavan Library, Chowk, Allahabad

A day in 1923.
The reading room is full.
In pin drop silence,
The regulars turn the pages
Of the morning papers.
One, a student, reaches for
A copy of the *Modern Review*,
Newly arrived.
At the issuing desk,
Some are borrowing books:
A detective novel in Urdu
In two volumes;
A free translation
Of a poem by Goldsmith
Printed in Etawah,
Titled *Yogi Arthur*.

The books
Are still on the shelves,
Their pages brittle
And spines missing.
New readers occupy the chairs,
Turning the pages
Of the morning papers.
Turning pages too,
But of dusty records
In a back room,
Is a researcher from Cambridge, England.
It's her second visit,
And everyone here knows her.

She's looking at Indian reading habits
In the colonial period.

Outside,
On the pavement,
Is a thriving vegetable market.
Amidst the stalls,
A knife-grinder sets up
His portable establishment
And opens for business.

Ironing Lady

Common everyday clothes,
Tied loosely in a bundle.
From it the ironing lady
Pulls out a kerchief
And glides the iron, its coals
Aglow, along the edges,
Making the creased valleys
Disappear under her hand.
A shirt's next. She begins

With the sleeves, then comes
To the craggy collar, then to
The plains of the front and back,
Slowing down as she
Nears the plastic buttons
And the wilderness
Between them. A pair
Of blue jeans is uphill
All the way. The iron hisses

And gets breathless
As she goes back and forth
Over the denim, occasionally
Wetting it with a damp rag.
In a corner of the table,
The ironed clothes pile up,
Each fold a stanza break,
Till she's folded the last one,
Finishing the manuscript.

Knife

He slapped his clothes,
Looked under the scales,
Rolled over the eggplants,
Poked the drumsticks.
Finally, spotting it,

The handle sticking out
From behind the cabbages,
He broke into a grin
As big as the one
He cut in the pumpkin
I'd asked a kilo of.

Ladies' Fingers

Go out and look
how old Mrs Hukkoo
picks ladies' fingers
with both hands.

She's so quick,
as if she's divined
before the cart's
inside the gate
where the smallest ones
are in the pile.

There's so much
to write about
but look at you.
All you do is to sit
at the computer all day
and stare at the screen.
Time's running out,
says my aproned wife,
wiping her onion tears
with the heel of her hand.

Egg Pedlar

'These could take all morning to sell,
Or could sell in minutes,' he said,
Pointing heavenward and lowering

The wicker basket from which he counted
A dozen free-range eggs for me. They looked
Like snub-nosed canon shells. He was old

And thin, and went from door to door
Announcing his ware, in his unknowing veins
The blood of Timurid kings.

Ear-Cleaning Man

Unlike the carder
And the caner,
The ear-cleaning man
Has no street cry.
To find him you
Only have to look
And he'll be there,
Sitting beside you
On upright crate
Or low wall, probing
Your waxy ear,
First one, then the other,
For you to hear
Your inner voice
The better with,
Before vanishing
As suddenly
As he'd appeared,
The hands free,
A small bag tucked
Under his arm,
And two needles
In his headband,
Like a pair of feelers.

Roadside Shrine

Before the padlocked
Businesses open for the day,
He sets up his shrine
To footwear: awl, rasp,

Hammer, tin of nails,
Nippers, cobbler's wax,
Thread, scissors, scraps
Of leather, bottle of

Glue. In the centre,
A cast iron anvil, a headless
God with two glib tongues,
The longer one sticking out,

Waiting for the day's first
Worshipper to bring
An offering of torn upper,
Worn heel, or flapping sole.

They'll Ride Out Any Storm

For the past five years,
From a market stall,
He's sold hand towels,
Bed linen, cheap ready-mades,
And Smiley wall hangings.

I've come to like this man.
From a passing cart
Laden with disco papayas,
He once helped me choose
A sweet one.

The last time I saw him
There was a summer
Dust storm blowing,
And while everyone else
Ran for cover,

He was fast asleep
On a pile
Of machine washable
Export quality
Scatter rugs.

Death in an Art Deco House

Forty-something, slight of build,
He lived next door with his parents
In an Art Deco house with a walled garden
And tall trees that came up to my third floor flat
From where I could touch their leaves. Squirrels
Ran up and down them all day, squeaking.

In a city he grew up in,
Which he'd never left, he had but
One friend, a retired bus driver who
Lived in a shack across the road, with whom
Most evenings he sat outside the house,
On a string cot, surrounded by street dogs
The colour of faded brown towels, the nap
Worn thin, and watched the world go by,
If only there'd been a world to go by.
Night comes suddenly in these latitudes.
Then, for no good reason, or none I know of,
He had the trees cut. I put up curtains
In the windows to keep out the morning sun
And forgot about the trees.

One hot afternoon
I saw rose petals scattered in the drive,
Some empty chairs, and melting blocks of ice.
I heard no crying.
Someone had died in the house
And been quietly cremated. The father, I thought,
Whom I'd see in the garden, the cord of his
Silk dressing gown firmly tied. Or maybe

The mother, who spent her mornings
Bent over the potted plants,
Removing the dead leaves. 'It was their son.
Surely you knew about him?' their old cook said
When I asked. 'No. Had he been ill?' He didn't
Answer my question, but closing the fingers
Of his right hand gestured towards his mouth
With his thumb. To be honest,
I'd forgotten about the squirrels too.

Koala Bear

It disappeared between
one birthday and the next,
the koala with brown glass eyes

that felt cold when touched.
I touched them often.
Its fur smelt of talcum.

All this was before
I drew the map freehand
and marked the rail-line

from Sydney to Perth.
A sucked thumb
is all that remains from that time.

Fears at Seven

Before going to bed
I struck the curtains
with a stick and hid
an open penknife
and a packet of sand
under the mattress.
But the minute it
was dark the ghostly
forms appeared. I heard
voices near the window,
whispers near the chair,
and looking for sunrise
shut my eyes tight.

Fears at Seventy

Annually, to show
I'm alive, I sign
at the pension office
a life certificate.
Crossing the road to
get there, I see a man
examining his tongue
in the rearview mirror
of a parked car. Is he
looking for signs of cancer?
No amount of sight,
hind, fore, or second, can
make unhappen the father
burying his son, parents
outliving their children.

Washing Tub

My hands bubble-wrapped in soapsuds,
I wash in a plastic tub a Sandow vest,
And hear on other terraces young mothers
Talking. It is morning and before me is open

The book of sunsets. I'll come
To the end of the page, and there aren't many
Pages remaining. How do I tell the mothers
It was a slim book to start with?

The Nest

With a menacing flutter
she who'd seen me handling
the dungy nest in the flowerpot
came and perched herself
on the empty deck chair
from where she could keep
a close eye on her two
beak-fed pigeon chicks
as I moved away and pretended
to look at the street below
where a servant-maid
was going to work carrying
at her hip her baby girl
whose head was covered
with a cotton cap printed
with small blue flowers.

Evening Walk

After a rubbish dump
And a country liquor bar,
The Adventist church,
A piglet in black
Ditch-water trousers
Running across its yard.

Further down the road,
A municipal tap. Under it,
Wielding a washing bat,
A woman beating
The life out of her clothes.
Then like a running sore

An open drain,
Sitting beside it two boys,
Bare-assed and swapping
Cricket stories while
Doing their business.
And the trees,

Let's not forget the trees.
Trapped in asphalt,
Their boles knobby with age,
Yet the sap pushing through
To gnarled branch, twig,
And erect bud

Year after year.

Night Vision

Last night,
Not far from where I live,
I was walking down a road alone.

Half the road was
Cordoned off for repairs
And shadowy figures,

Covered in dust,
Sat crouched over wire brushes,
Cleaning its surface,

Or fetched boiling
Tar from a drum,
To sprinkle on potholes

Filled evenly with broken stones.
In a house across the road,
Where I'd played as a child,

I saw blue flowers,
Each the size
Of a beach umbrella,

With a transparent stem. Behind me,
I heard a car stop
And a woman I knew,

Who looked to be in mourning,
Was walking towards me.
I was afraid,

But before I could run
Or wake up,
She'd done her job.

The Sting in the Tail

Wearing loose clothes, light cottons,
You sit and fan yourself with a newspaper
Supplement, a glass of tepid
Fennel-flavoured sherbet by your side.

From the window you see
A car turn, a bus pass, or a cyclist,
A towel wrapped around his head.
It's 45 degrees centigrade

In the shade, and according to the forecast
There's worse to come.
A neighbour's genset
Sputters in the background.

At night, still without electricity,
In the sooty warm light of a kerosene lamp,
You read John Ashbery and thwack!
That was a fat mosquito

Leaving your forearm.

Summer Break

Back in the old house,
But I'm not back there yet,
And won't be until June,
In the summer break.

The litchis will still be green,
Hanging low in the trees,
In bunches, or hanging
High, unreachable, but not safe,

When they redden, from
The prying eyes,
The plucking arms of schoolboys.
The mangos, hard as stones,

Aimed stones will find;
They'll fall unbruised, sour.
Some, suspended on long
Stems, will survive, ripen,

To be raided by waves of
Shrieking fruit bats, swooping
Down. I'll be there,
Not to chase them away

But survey the night's damage
In the morning. Then there are
Termites, secretive, shy,
Multiplying like cancer cells

In doorframes and windowsills.
It's a losing battle,
If it was ever joined.
To have another day to wake up to,

Small birds chittering on the roof,
The ice cream cart going by,
The leaves silvery in the light,
Never ceases to surprise.

Number 16

Where your neighbour has built his garage
Was the tennis court, and to the right
Of the streetlight on Old Survey Road
The main gate. It was sold as scrap,
For almost nothing. I was born here, in
Number 16, and know this property,
Every pit and slope, like the back of my hand.
Tenants lived in the main house then
And your uncle, who came to escape
The heat of Allahabad, was a summer visitor.
He stayed in the same rooms
You stay in now. The ten weeks he spent here
Passed quickly. He suffered from this strange
Disease as you know and couldn't
Eat his food or comb his hair unaided.
He went everywhere in a wheelchair,
That one of us had to push.
I was just a boy then, and my job was
To sit by his desk, on a high stool, and turn
The pages of the book he was reading.
They seemed like old books, for their pages
Were brittle and I had to be careful turning them.
He once scolded me for some mischief I'd done,
But the next day he sent for me and apologized.
I won't ever forget that. My friends and I
Played hooky from school and came here.
There were always rocks on the ground, fruit
Above, and my arm never failed me.
If I told you the names of the mango
Varieties we had here you'd think I was

Speaking from an imaginary textbook
On horticulture. You call these trees?
They're dwarfs compared to those giants,
Whose yield we sold by the cartload,
On the sly. You were our masters, but we
Had the run of the land. We couldn't have
Survived on my father's salary otherwise.
Eleven rupees a month it was, and
Never a paisa's raise, till the day he died.
The eviction suit you brought against
The tenants dragged on for twelve years.
Seeing that my father was getting old
And had no savings to speak of,
They once offered him money
To change his testimony in court.
But we'd eaten your salt and couldn't do that.
Eventually, they lost the case. The land
Got sold, your uncle died, and the house
Was divided. I was the one who
Put up the new boundary wall.
But the bad days lay still ahead. They came
After your father's suicide, when your mother
Went to work in a school. The garden, or
What was left of it, became a jungle.
At night, bats flew about in the rooms.
Termite ants ate through the doorframes.
We servants lived in the outhouses at the back,
Without electricity. My sister lived
With us, along with her good-for-nothing son.
But it was Noma, the young sweeperess,
Who gave us untold trouble. She
Took up with Ratan, who was a bad sort.
One day two men, a third was in the getaway

Auto-rickshaw parked at a distance, came
Looking for her. It was pitch dark. I could smell
The alcohol on their breath before I could see
Their faces. Where's Noma? one of them asked,
Putting a gun to my chest. I don't know,
I said, smoke coming out of my ass.
He poked me in the ribs and repeated
The question. My sister must have heard us,
For she came out and stood in the door.
She saw the two men, she saw the gun, and
She saw me. She let out an almighty scream.
She was a big woman. The two men fled,
But before that we'd fled ourselves, disappeared
Into the bushes, which were everywhere.
We spent the night hiding in them, too scared
To come out. The next morning we trooped off
To your mother's school and gave her an account
Of the night's events. We told her we weren't
Ready to mind this place in her absence
Any more. Noma, who'd seen everything
From her room, came with us. A few weeks later,
The police laid a trap and got Ratan.
He was killed right here, where the jackfruit tree is.
The news was all over town and in the papers.
You see these walls. They're twenty-four inches
Thick, and you're worried about the house falling.
It's good for another generation at least.
As someone who's repaired it
Times without number, I should know.

Herodotus, My Mother, and Civets

There are no gold-digging ants here,
Or trees that bear wool instead of fruit,
Or men whose ears reach to their feet.
But I have seen my mother recently,
Her remembering head thrown back,
Having oil rubbed in her thinning white hair,
And at night heard the civets, come out to forage.
Woken up by a banging on the roof,
I saw their silhouettes, as they stood
On the storage tank, the moon behind them.

The Meal

You know the game's up
When the house you live in
Begins to eat you.

The timbered roof
Is the roof of its mouth,
The pitted stone floor

Its rotted teeth,
The front and back doors
Its knife and fork

Cutting you into small pieces.
You look up from the plate
Towards the Belling

On the sideboard
Where your mother is standing
Inside a walker,

An unpaid bill
In her hand,
Supervising the meal.

In a Greek City

Egypt, 315

Bringing my face up against hers,
'Who am I?' I say to my mother.
She's sitting on the edge of the bed,
Her legs swollen, stiff, the colour of white stone.
'Neilos,' she says, 'but why do you ask?'
Her big eyes, wide open, stare at me
Uncomprehendingly. 'Can't find my comb,' she says.
'Have you seen it?' Her right arm's in plaster.
The wind, sand-filled, blows through the house, rattling
Windows, opening and closing the unhinged
Panels of her mind. I give her the comb.
In a gesture I know so well, her left palm,
Bent at the knuckle, touches the hairline,
Ready to follow the comb's path through the tangles,
But the hand has no grip and the comb slips.
Shoulders hunched, hands in her lap, she looks
Like a child abandoned in a park.
'Let it be, we'll do the hair later,'
I tell her and go upstairs to get her breakfast –
A cup of milk, honey-cake, figs.
She eats hungrily, and I watch her eat,
Wiping her gummy mouth from time to time.
A sweet-talker with one sharp tongue, she spoke
In many voices; neighbours and slaves
Told her their stories; she was the keeper
Of gossip. No one now comes, except
The wind blows, the windows rattle, and she asks,
'Where's Mama? Where's Papa? Where are my sisters?'
'They're dead,' I tell her, matter of factly,
As though reporting an incident in the street.

'Is that so,' she says, her mind somewhere else.
'Get me something to eat. What do we have?'
'But you've just eaten. See, you forget.'
She forgets that she forgets.
'Whose house is this?' she asks. 'Where's my bedroom?
When are we going back to Number 16?'
'You're in your own house,' I tell her.
'You're in Number 16, where you've always lived.
Don't you recognize the garden? the stairs?
The Gospels on the shelf, Matthew and John?
Shall I read out a passage?' She looks tired.
I ask her to walk, to get some exercise,
But she's adamant. 'My no's a no.'
That's more like her. When she lies down, on her side,
I roll up her vest, exposing her back,
Letting the disinfecting sun fall directly
On her skin, where it's discoloured, purplish, hard,
One unhealing bedsore oozing thickly.

Construction Site

It went on all morning,
The sound of axe on wood,
Followed by the sound
Of a branch creaking.

High up on a neem tree
I spotted him, T-shirted,
A week's stubble on his chin,
An axe in his hand.

The tree stood
On the edge of our land.
He saw me too; then,
Wiping his face,

Spat to one side
And cautioned his mate
As a branch came
Crashing down. Limbless

And bare, its twisted leaves
Like a wreath at its foot,
The tree looked
Like a war memorial.

By evening even this was gone,
Leaving, where the crown was,
A neat hole in the sky,
As though made by a bullet.

Machete

A few blows of the machete
And the young tree
Lay sprawled on the ground.

Dragging it across the yard,
I almost didn't see the nest,
Its leaves joined as firmly

As bricks. It looked warm,
Habitable, like the house I entered
To put away the machete

In a table drawer, muttering
'Sorry, bird' to no one in particular
As I did so.

Hedge Scissors

As I climbed down the ladder,
Pruning the honeysuckle
That winds up the front wall
Like a mountain road, I came
In a bend in the stem
To a cross-hatch of twigs,
Like a squatter's shack.
It was empty.

Only someone who's stepped on
A garden snail and felt
The soft crunch underfoot,
Will know how it was
When, later, while collecting
The refuse, I saw the bird's egg
In the unmown grass,
Its white shell cracked and gluey,
With a trace of red.

Picking Pole

The Rangoon creeper,
One pinkish leg
Over the parapet, waits
To sneak into the house,
And perched on the water-butt,
Facing the mountains,
The magpie robin
Raises an alarm.
Singly, in pairs, babblers
Hop in the shingle patch,
Eating their breakfast of insects.
I'm outside, watching them
From the mango trees
Bordering the lawn,
A picking pole in my hand,
The weeds ankle high,
Some of the fruit, bird eaten,
Rotting on the ground,
The seed, white,
Showing through the pulp
Like a newborn's skull,
On a morning in late summer
Of my sixtieth year.

Looking Out

The strings of water beads, after a shower,
On leafless willow branches; the squirrels
On the verandah, hopping, pausing,
Racing up the iron ladder to the roof,
Several times a day; four parrots flying
In air show formation, leaving vapour trails;
The spotted owlet in the mango tree,
Looking in through the open window where I
Sit at a jade table looking out, in a house
Where nothing happens that so much happens
You can't close your eyes for a sec.

Implements

On the shingles,
the same colour as its fur,
a cat's cut-out.

Shovelled off the ground
and tossed into an empty
cement bag, it is carried

to a corner of the garden
and there left
on a mound of trash.

3 kilos of dead cat,
its head an unsightly red,
is in that bag

that looks like any other.
As does the shovel,
after the blood's

been hosed off it
and it stands in the garden shed
next to a rake.

Guava Tree

Parrots know
better than me

the guavas on
my guava tree.

In Midair

On seeing it hanging
from a branch
of the cotton tree,
its wing-tip snagged
on a kite string,
my first thought was
that it's a pigeon.
I took it for dead
when our eyes met

and with a long pole,
an angled peg
twined to one end,
I tugged at the string
and saw the owl
flutter down to settle
on a stump in
the undergrowth,
its first blink coming
after ten of mine.

Explosion

An explosion in the garden.
I stretched my neck out and looked.
Fantails screaming in the mulberry tree,
The leaves flecked with dried blood.

Two nights ago, the verbal knives out,
Rust free and vowel-edged, we'd screamed too,
Just like these birds, and like them
We'd stopped, as suddenly as we'd begun.

The clothes on the clothesline have dried, love.
It's time to bring them in.
No sounds come from the mulberry
Fruiting in the midday sun.

'As crazed yellow butterflies'

As crazed yellow butterflies
Thronged the young willow
In the garden
And the clean morning light
Cut through the fruit trees
Like a knife,
The old spider,
From his hummock
In the verandah,
His fangs on the ready,
Through the camouflage
Of leaves and ropey stalks
Of potted climbers,
Looked on.

Growing Chillies

In summer
we grow chillies.

We make finger holes
in the wet soil
and put in the saplings,
careful to keep the hosepipe
away from the roots
or the saplings keel over.
The stone-bordered level
ground in which they grow
is their playground.

This year we lost all our plants.
They were healthy one week,
looked ill the next.
Friends would remark,
What's wrong with your chillies?

The plants were young,
and we too old to care,
or care too much.
We let them go.
One step wide
and two across,
this small piece of earth
is the whole of it.

Hoopoe

Who remembers my dentist father
Now that even his patients are dead.
A hoopoe pecks at the sodden ground
Beside the latched gate, on which is hung
A rusted signboard with his name and
Clinic hours, the letters illegible
And getting more so. Like a spark
Of fire in the air, the hoopoe's
Vanished into the trees, leaving the patch
Of earth a little dark where it came
Looking for grubs. It's been raining.
We belong to the houses we live in.

My Father's Tootal Ties

My father's Tootal ties
slip from the rack
when I open the cupboard.
Unworn for decades,
they're as good as new.
He was a fashionable man.

Back of the house
is a pomegranate tree.
In driest summer – when the only
thing to thrive is the marijuana plant
which in any case grows wild
in the valley – the pomegranate
puts forth at the end of a slender branch
two testicular fruit, the first
of the season. They fall before
they ripen, their thin skins bitten away
by squirrels, their pinkish interior
anatomical to look at.

I hear bird sounds everywhere,
hooraying and cheering from
window ledge, water tank, and scrub
as the year's longest day passes
as quickly as the shortest.

My Mother's New Bras

The old pomegranate, storm-hit, propped up
with sticks, sends out a green shoot that goes
straight and up from the root but brings
no hope for the stricken tree. It's the same

for my ninety-year-old mother.
Broken-boned, assisted out of bed, she
goes to the mirrored cupboard, straightens her
back, and takes a long look at herself. Secretly,

she once sent for some cotton bras that
turned out to be a few sizes too big and were
later found among her urinous clothes,
unworn, stiff, in their original folds.

Seven Sisters

They sounded like hens cackling,
The Seven Sisters in the pine tree,
Shouting at the top of their voices,
As more birds joined them, some
From the vicinity, others that were
Passing by. Then all was quiet again.

Once the countdown's begun,
The days passing more quickly,
The long quiet approaching,
It's not quiet you want but the quiet
To shatter, the unmelodious birds back,
Their throats on fire.

Paradise Flycatcher

This unkept,
Dark-shadowed garden,
With its bamboo stand,
Silver oak and pine,

Was their place of
Assignation, their
Neon-lit mall, cinema
Hall, and restaurant, their

Car park and bus stop,
Sometimes their hotel room
And back seat of a taxi.
They chased each other

Through our trees
And our neighbours',
Unvictimized, unnoticed,
No boundary fence

Stopping them, no feathered
Father or brother
Beheading them in the street
In an honour killing.

Bird Book

I
Looking like the 65th species
of heron, egret, and bittern
in the Made in Cambodia

t-shirt she calls Tacky White,
making it sound like the name
of a butterfly in *Speak, Memory*,

she stood hunchbacked
under the eucalyptus
in which a cattle egret

in breeding plumage
was hiding in the leaves,
its bill turned

towards a frog pond, as though
from its slime will appear
fair Lancelot or Lochinvar.

II
Available for sale or rent
with sunset and mountain views,
hand-built single home
set amidst litchi trees,
eco-friendly using 100%
pine needles, lightweight,
cup shaped, the rim wide
then narrowing, the walls thick,
the base deep; attached to it
a twig and a piece of string,
white, belonging to a black
garbage bag being used
for the disposal of adult
diapers, medium sized.

Car access, wifi,
caretaker present 24/7.
Suitable for a small bird
in the family way.

III

A widow sits under
a spruce tree
and reads her beloved Kafka.
Today, it is 'A Dream'.
She's in the hills
and the sky is hazy.
She hears a bird
and calls it a bell-bird,
for it makes a sound
like the bell-bird in Bundoora.

She's only 60
and thinks she'll remarry
if she can find someone
like her late husband who,
unknown to her, would
gently raise the pillow
on which she slept and kiss
the thin line of her lips.

She looks up from the page.
There's a motley crew of birds
shrieking at the gate.

Worker Ant

The few things it needs lie within
Walking distance: an insect wing,
A grain of sugar. Sometimes it takes
A Grand Tour of roadside litter,
Or goes hiking alone in shingle
Mountains, past thumbnail lakes.
Its happiest moments are at a jungle
Boot camp, crawling on twigs,
Struggling in a bog-hole under
The garden tap, pushing a grass blade
Ten times its size towards a towering
Clod of earth in the flowerbed.
I saw the grass move before I saw
Its mover, hiding in plain sight.

Squirrel

Hidden behind fronds,
it sat on the Chinese
fan palm, pulling out
with its paws
fibres I first thought
it was eating, when it
pulled out some more
like it was someone's
hair and ran along
the boundary wall
to where its nest was,
carrying the building
material in its mouth.

The Dispersed Library

His vision poor,
his library dispersed,
the cell phone's buttons

hard to read.
On empty shelves
appeared pagan scrolls

licked by Christian fires,
illuminated lives
skinned alive

by Khalji swords,
a grammarian's flame
Sinhalese guns put out.

Dark as the rum
he poured himself,
the night fell.

Number 16 Revisited

This was Anna Villa
bought from the Lumsdens
ninety years ago.
The table I sit at
came with the house
and is still serviceable.
The house itself has fared less well.
It is coming apart at the joints
like its three inhabitants.
From checkerboard tile floor to timbered ceiling
earthquake cracks widen
along thick mud and stone walls.
The flat roof sags and the batten wiring with it.
When it rains the roof leaks.
It rains all the time.
Beyond the straw gods
is my unheavenly kingdom,
the house I'm always coming back to,
manuring the land
with the ash of burnt leaves,
turning the soil with a broken bean-stick,
chronicling its life with a stick of lead.

The House I Live In

Brick dust and the chunks
of lime mortar that fall
from damp wall, arch,
and ceiling I sweep into a pan

and scatter them like
ashes over the garden weeds,
burying the house I live in
in the house I live in.

Grass-Cutter

To fodder her goats
she comes for what weeds
the garden provides
her lightning-edged sickle.

Forward, sideways,
she moves on her haunches,
rising only to leave,
a bundle on her head,
looking taller than before.

Oink!

Oink! Said one,
Oink! Said the other,
Oink! They said together,
Ambling down
The middle of the lane,
When a passing dog,
All bark no bite,
Chased them towards a wall,
Along which they ran,
Snouts to the ground,
Bellies wobbling,
Rounding the corner so fast
They almost fell off
Their pig legs,
Their oinks becoming
Honks as they merged
Into the traffic.

Homo Naledi

It's nice to read about them
though they're no relations of mine,
the Homo naledi found in a cave
near Jo'burg, their bones displayed
like necklace beads on blue velvet.

The hominins I'm interested in
belong to more recent times,
solid middle class folk –
school teachers, record keepers, tradesmen –
ground into the dust of the Punjab plains
and leaving no trace.

The Nulla-Nulla in Nullah

There's ire in fire, a ban in turban,
A rind in tamarind, a listen in glisten,
A reed in greedy, umber in lumber,
And the other way round.

There's a vine in divine, a pot in potato,
Oggle in goggle, rang in boomerang,
A miss in mission, an ate in plate,
And the other way round.

There's a tick in tickle, a rift in drift,
A trap in trapeze, a feat in defeat,
A bed in bedraggled, timbre in timbrel,
And the other way round.

There's riot in patriot, Zen in citizen,
A give in forgive, a wig in wigwam,
An amp in lamp, a 'Sh!' in shooter,
And the other way round.

There's a pie in magpie, a fad in fade,
A cab in caboose, the ark in lark,
There's old in gold, an Om in doom,
And the other way round.

There's a jin in jinricksha, a cry in descry,
A sire in desire, a rob in Robin Hood,
There's other in mother, size in capsize,
And the other way round.

There's laughter in slaughter, a hind in Hindoo,
A hare in harem, a hound in Mahound,
A pig in pigeon, an ear in hear,
And the other way round.

There's rust in trust, a vark in aard-vark,
Goo in goo-goo, nulla-nulla in nullah,
A come in income tax, a gent in Gentoo,
And the other way round.

There's tawny in mulligatawny, a ling in lingerie,
An end in endoscopy, an Abba in Abbot,
A squirr in squirrel, a devi in devil,
And the other way round, and the other way round.

Translations

from

The Absent Traveller

Prakrit Love Poetry from the
Gāthāsaptaśatī of Satavahana Hala

(1991)

Written in Maharashtri Prakrit, the *Gāthāsaptaśatī* (700 Verses in the *gatha* form) or *Gāhākōsō* (A Treasury of Gathas) is perhaps the earliest anthology of secular Indian verse, and dates from the 1st–2nd century CE. This is only a century after the Greek poet Meleager of Gadara put together the *Stephanos* ('Garland'), which became the model of what we now know as the *Greek Anthology*. Both anthologies have had a lasting influence on their region's literatures. Even a thousand years after it was compiled, by the Satavahana king Hala, the *Gāthāsaptaśatī*'s verses were being quoted in works of Sanskrit poetics, where they appear as examples of rhetorical techniques and to explicate the functions of *dhvani* or 'resonance'.

As many as half the *Gāthāsaptaśatī*'s verses are assigned to individual poets, a handful of whom are women. Unfortunately, we know nothing else about them. The speakers of the poems, though, are almost solely women, and they are of all ages, from an ingénue (verses 123, 145, 155) to an ancient crone, reminiscing about her past affairs (verses 239, 372, 518). Among the few poems where a man is the speaker are verses 23, 52, and, perhaps, 427.

In their choice of dramatis personae, mood, and love situation, the *gathas* bear a striking resemblance to the Tamil *akam* anthologies of the Cankam period (with which they were contemporaneous) as well as to Sanskrit poetry. See A.K. Ramanujan, *The Interior Landscape: Classical Tamil Love Poems* (New York: NYRB/Poets, 2013) and Martha Ann Selby, *Grow Long Blessed Night: Love Poems from Classical India* (New York: Oxford University Press, 2000). The numbers following the poems are according to Albrecht Weber's *Das Saptaçatakam des Hāla* (Leipzig: F.A. Brockhaus, 1881).

At night, cheeks blushed
    With joy, making me do
A hundred different things,
    And in the morning too shy
To even look up. I don't believe
    It's the same woman.

23

After a quarrel,
    The breath suppressed,
Their ears attentive,
    The lovers feign sleep:
Let's see who
    Holds out longer.

27

Lives in main street,
    Attractive, young, her husband away,
A light wench her neighbour, hard up too,
    And, unbelievably, still chaste.

36

Afraid of midday heat,
    Even your shadow
Stays under your feet:
    Come into the shade, traveller.

49

Hair like ruffed feathers,
    Half open eyes,
The body in tremors needing rest:
    Having played the man,
You now know how we suffer.

                                                    52

The way he stared,
    I kept covering myself,
Not that I wanted him
    To look elsewhere.

                                                    73

Distance destroys love,
So does the lack of it.

Gossip destroys love,
And sometimes

It takes nothing
To destroy love.

                                                    81

In her first labour,
    She tells her friends,
'I won't let him
    Touch me again.' They laugh.

                                                    123

His form
    In my eyes,
His touch
    In my limbs,
His words
    In my ears,
His heart
    In my heart:
Now who's
    Separated?

                                                132

'A safflower!' they shouted,
    Pointing to the nail-mark
On her breast, and laughed
    When she tried to brush it.

                                                145

Ignorant of how it ends,
    The bride, having come,
Looks up as if to say
    'Go on.'

                                                155

As the traveller, eyes raised,
    Cupped hands filled with water, spreads
His fingers and lets it run through,
    She pouring it reduces the trickle.

                                                161

To keep from spiteful tongues
    Her love for you,
She looks at everyone
    With equal affection.

                                          199

From the river thicket
    Where it saw a girl deflowered,
The astonished flock rose
    With a shudder.

                                          218

A scorpion's bitten her,' they cried,
    And as she thrashed about,
Her shrewd friends in her husband's presence
    Rushed her to her physician lover.

                                          237

It's no untruth:
    My death-bed's
Near the sacred waters
    Of the Tapi,

And the eye
    Roves over
That thicket
    Just as before.

                                          239

Bookish lovemaking
Is soon repetitive.
It's the improvised style
Wins my heart.

274

She thrusts her lover
    Towards her husband back early:
'This man just arrived
    From my father's village.'

301

Unable to count
    The days of separation
Beyond her fingers and toes,
    The unlettered girl broke down.

307

Promises
    Not to bite
The underlip,

The lamp
    Puffed out,
The speech
    A whisper,
And the breath
    Confined

Make forbidden love
    Felicitous.

333

He groped me
　　For the underwear
That wasn't
　　There:

I saw the boy's
　　Fluster
And embraced him
　　More tightly.

　　　　　　　　　　　　　　　351

O hideous old age,
　　Be content. I've come
To worship the stone
　　Men used for my pillow.

　　　　　　　　　　　　　　　372

Fore-legs positioned on the bank,
　　Hinders agitating in the ripples,
The she-frog strokes her own reflection.

　　　　　　　　　　　　　　　391

We're trugs all right
　　And you're a paragon,
But at least we don't
　　Fantasize chiropodists.

　　　　　　　　　　　　　　　417

Like two noble warriors
    Laid low in close combat,
Your breasts even fallen
    Look handsome.

                                        427

'What's this?'
    She innocently wonders,
And now washes, now rubs, now scratches
    The nail-mark on her breast.

                                        433

He finds the missionary position
    Tiresome, and grows suspicious
If I suggest another.
    Friend, what's the way out?

                                        476

In the last weeks
    Of pregnancy

She's distressed by
    Her inability

To mount him.

                                        483

Those men,
      This once rich village,
And days of my youth

Are now stories
      That sometimes
Reach my ears too.

                                                    518

The lamp-oil finished,
      The wick still burns,
Engrossed in the young couple's
      Copulation.

                                                    548

The cock crows and you
      Wake up with a start.
But you've spent the night
      In your own bed, husband.

                                                    583

All he wants
      Is to see her armpit,
So asks the garland-maker
      The price of a string.

                                                    599

Deerslayer
    Aiming at doe.

Doe's eyes
    Fixed on a stag.

Deerslayer
    Remembers his wife.

Deerslayer's bow
    Drops.

                                        620

As the bridegroom
    Feigning sleep
Sidles towards her,
    Her thighs stiffen and swiftly
With trembling hand
    She clasps the knot.

                                        648

Always wanting me
    To come on top
And complaining
    We're childless.
As if you can fill
    An inverted water jug.

                                        656

To bandits
    Lovers
Travellers
    The cock cries:

Loot
    Copulate
Speed well
    The night flies.

701

Troubled by thoughts
    Of his desolate wife,
The absent traveller
    Now approaches his village,
Now leaves it behind.

707

Proud, aren't you, to display
    The beauty streaks
Your husband's painted on your breasts?

When I stood before mine,
    His hand lost all
Control over the line.

830

Let faithful wives
    Say what they like,
I don't sleep with my husband
    Even when I do.

888

from

Songs of Kabir

(2011)

Of all north Indian poets, past or present, perhaps no one is more readily quoted than Kabir. His verses are sung from Bengal to Rajasthan, and as far south as the Malwa region of Madhya Pradesh. It is another matter that of not one of the thousands of verses ascribed to him can it be said with any certainty that he is their author. In fact, their very anonymity holds the key to their diffusion. To this day, anyone who writes a Kabirian poem attributes it in the signature line to this 15th century Bhakti poet. Born in Benaras into a family of weavers, Kabir chose to die not in the holy city of his birth but, in keeping with his contrarian views, in the miasmic village of Maghar, about which the legend was that those who die there are reborn as asses.

A lifelong hater of sham, Kabir believed in a personal god and satirised both caste-marked temple-going Hindus and mosque-going Turks, his word for Muslims. He referred to his god sometimes as Rama and sometimes as Hari, neither of whom is to be confused with Hindu gods of the same name.

The best Kabir editions currently available are based on an assortment of manuscripts or manuscript traditions, whose compilers, from the mid-sixteenth century onwards, would have either heard the songs themselves or copied them from existing written sources. Since no two singers sang the same song, making changes and improvising as the mood took them, the songs have reached us in several versions. Further changes would have been introduced by the compilers or even by the scribes, all of which goes to make the Kabir text a scholarly minefield.

The number following the poem indicates the number of the poem in these editions: *Kabir-granthavali*, edited by Parasnath Tiwari (Allahabad: Hindi Parishad, 1961), abbreviated as KG; *Kabir-granthavali,* edited by Mata Prasad Gupta (Allahabad: Sahitya Bhavan, 1969), abbreviated as KGG; *Kabir-vangmay*, edited by Jaydev Singh and Vasudev Singh (Varanasi: Vishwavidyalaya Prakashan, 1981), abbreviated as KV.

Listen carefully,
Neither the Vedas
Nor the Qur'an

Will teach you this:
Put the bit in its mouth,

The saddle on its back,
Your foot in the stirrup,

And ride your wild runaway mind
All the way to heaven.

KG 81

I'd say this
Through a megaphone
If I had one:

Look at these men.
Shaven heads,
Great big earrings,
Ash-smeared bodies,
But inside they're empty
As a house that's been
Cleaned out by thieves.

And look at these others
In the best part of town,
Who forget that when death
Slips its noose round their necks
To drag them through the streets
It won't be pretty.

I live in Fearlessburg,
Kabir the weaver says.
Its builder? Rama.

KG 170

If going naked
Brought liberation,
The deer of the forest
Would attain it first.

If a shaven head
Was a sign of piety,
Ewes would be
Pious too.

If holding back the semen
Brought you closer to heaven,
A steer would
Lead the way.

There's no salvation
Without Rama, says Kabir.
Not to know it is
Really dumb.

KG 174

To tonsured monks and dreadlocked Rastas,
To idol worshippers and idol smashers,
To fasting Jains and feasting Shaivites,
To Vedic pundits and Faber poets,
The weaver Kabir sends one message:
The noose of death hangs over all.
Only Rama's name can save you.
Say it NOW.

                                              KG 85

It take a man that have the blues so to sing the blues.
LEADBELLY

O pundit, your hairsplitting's
So much bullshit. I'm surprised
You still get away with it.

If parroting the name
Of Rama brought salvation,
Then saying *sugarcane*
Should sweeten the mouth,
Saying *fire* burn the feet,
Saying *water* slake thirst,
And saying *food*
Would be as good as a belch.

If saying *money* made everyone rich,
There'd be no beggars in the streets.

My back is turned on the world,
You hear me singing of Rama and you smile.
One day, Kabir says,
All bundled up,
You'll be delivered to Deathville.

KG 179

Were the Creator
Concerned about caste,
We'd arrive in the world
With a caste mark on the forehead.

If you say you're a Brahmin
Born of a mother who's a Brahmin,
Was there a special canal
Through which you were born?

And if you say you're a Turk
And your mother's a Turk,
Why weren't you circumcised
Before birth?

Nobody's lower-caste;
The lower castes are everywhere.
They're the ones
Who don't have Rama on their lips,

Kabir says.

KG 182

Running up minarets,
Calling out to the faithful
Five times a day,
What's your problem, muezzin?

Can't you see you're a walking
Mosque yourself?
Your mind's your Mecca;
Your body the Ka'aba
That you face when you pray;
Anything you say
Is an utterance from heaven.
Cut the throat of desire,
Not a poor goat's, if you must.

Kabir says, I'm possessed,
Just don't ask me how
It happened or when.

KG 129

for Geoff Dyer

his front yard / is the true Benares
    Devara Dasimayya (10th century), v. 98
    Trans. A.K. Ramanujan

His death in Benares
Won't save the assassin
From certain hell,

Any more than a dip
In the Ganges will send
Frogs – or you – to paradise.

My home, says Kabir,
Is where there's no day, no night,
And no holy book in sight

To squat on our lives.

                              KG 84

Separate us?
Pierce a diamond first.

We're lotus
And water,
Servant
And master.
My love for you
Is no secret.

I'm the grub
To your ichneumon fly,

The river
To your sea,

The borax
To your gold,

Heightening its effect.

KG 18

Tell me, wise one,
How did I become
A woman from a man?

I never got married,
Was never pregnant,
But gave birth to sons.

I fucked young men,
Too numerous to count,
And stayed a virgin.

In a Brahmin's house,
I become a Brahmin's wife;
In a yogi's, a lay yogini;

In a Turk's, I read the *kalma*
And do as Turkish women do;
And yet I'm always alone

Without a place to call home.
Listen, saints, Kabir says,
This is my body.

I don't let
My husband touch it
Or anyone else.

KG 160

god my darling
do me a favour and kill my mother-in-law
        JANABAI (13th century) Trans. ARUN KOLATKAR

Chewing slowly,
Only after I'd eaten
My grandmother,
Mother,
Son-in-law,
Two brothers-in-law,
And father-in-law
(His big family included)
In that order,
And had for dessert
The town's inhabitants,

Did I find, says Kabir,
The beloved that I've become
One with.

                          KGG 3.25

Those who are not
Devotees of Rama
Should be in Sing Sing
Or have been stillborn.

Better their mothers
Had been widows
Or barren
Than to have given birth
To these smartly dressed
Pigs who, lacking Rama,
Are like cripples

In rags.

KG 64

I've dyed myself
In the colour of Rama;
It's the only dye
That doesn't spoil or run.

All the others, says Kabir,
Fade in the sun,
Like a kite on a string
Growing faint in the sky.

KV 259

And what was yesterday a little mucus,
tomorrow will be a mummy or ashes.
      Marcus Aurelius, *Meditations*, IV. 48

Birth is scented with death.
      Bhartrihari (c. 5th century), v. 197
      Trans. Barbara Stoler Miller

Friend,
You had one life,
And you blew it.

From sticky spunk
To human shape,
You spent ten months

In your mother's womb,
Blocked off from the world
Into which you fell

The minute you were born.
A child once,
You're an old man now.

What has happened has happened.
Crying won't help
When death already

Has you by the balls.
It's counting your breaths,
Waiting.

This world, says Kabir,
Is a gambling den.
You can't be too careful.

KG 60

A light skiff will put out, you will be on it –
and, win the pools, you still will go aboard.
        Horace, *Ode* II.14, Trans. C.H. Sisson

Easy, friend.
What's the big fuss about?

Once dead,
The body that was stuffed with
Kilos of sweets
Is carried out to be burnt,
And the head on which
A bright turban was tied
Is rolled by crows in the dust.
A man with a stick
Will poke the cold ashes
For your bones.

But I'm wasting my time,
Says Kabir.
Even death's bludgeon
About to crush your head
Won't wake you up.

                                        KG 62

Uncollected Translations

Nirala

Breaking Stones

Beside a road in Allahabad,
I saw her
    breaking stones.

No tree to give her shade,
A dark skin,
Firm, tightly-cupped breasts,
Eyes fixed on the ground,
Thoughts of the night before
Going through her mind,
She brought down the heavy hammer
Again and again, as though it was
A weapon in her hand.
Across the road –
A row of trees, high walls,
The mansions of the rich.

The sun climbed the sky.
The height of summer.
Blinding heat, and the *loo* blowing hard,
Scorching everything in its path.
The earth under the feet
Like burning cotton wool,
The air filled with dust and sparks.
It was almost noon,
And she was still breaking stones.

As I watched,
She looked at me once,
Then at the houses opposite,
Then at her ragged clothes.

Seeing there was no one around,
She met my eyes again
With eyes that spoke of pain
But not defeat.

Suddenly, there came the notes of a sitar,
Such as I had not heard before.
The next moment her young body
Quivered and as sweat
Trickled down her face, she lifted
The hammer, resuming work,
As though to say,
    I'm breaking stones.

April 4, 1937

Love Song

I'm a Brahmin's son,
But have fallen
    for this girl.

A potter's daughter
We've hired to fetch water,
She comes every morning at the crack of dawn.
She's the one I'm after.

Black as a koel,
No curves to her figure,
Of marriageable age
But not yet married.
That's what did it,
    and a sigh escaped me.

Her loud knock on the door
Wakes up the house.
No one else knows what's going on.
She takes the water-pot,
The big one, and steps out again,
My eyes following her.
    I haven't lost heart.

February 22, 1939

Little Princess, or The One-Eyed Girl

Her mother calls her Little Princess,
Affectionately, as the name suggests.
The truth, however,
Is a pock-pitted, flat-nosed, bald,
And one-eyed face.

    Little Princess has come of age.
    She cuts and threshes, pounds and grinds,
    Trims the wickers till her hands are raw,
    Sweeps the floor, throws the rubbish out,
    Fills the pots with water.

Still, her mother's heart is troubled.
It feels like a box a thief has emptied.
Where will she get
A husband for her daughter?
She despairs if someone
Says in the neighbourhood,

    'All said and done,
    Little Princess is a woman.
    Who wants a one-eyed wife?'
    When Little Princess hears this

Her body shivers.
She sees her mother's grief
And a tear fills her good eye.
But the blind left one
Stays dry, alert.

1939

Moscow Dialogues

My new friend Gidwani
Is a big socialist.
He's come to see me with a copy of *Moscow Dialogues*.
'This is *Moscow Dialogues*,' he says, smiling.
Subhas Babu* had sent for it in jail.
He gave it to me at a resort where we met.
Till '35 there were barely two copies of the book
In this backward country.'
Then he says, 'My brother's building a house,
The work needs to be supervised,
It doesn't leave me with time for much else.'
Then he says, 'There are some rich people here,
All of them fools, and one bigger than the other,
But they don't easily write cheques.
They need to be tackled somehow.
I've finished a novel.
Do take a look.
If it's published the cretins will be impressed
And I can get them to part with their money again.
The idea is to move into a big house and start a printing business.
You're welcome to come and stay with me if you wish.
It'll be a comfortable life.'
I flip through the novel.
Its misspelt opening words are
'My drearest sweatest Syama, I'm in lov.'
I put it down, look at *Moscow Dialogues*,
Look at Gidwani.

1940

*Subhas Chandra Bose.

'All alone'

All alone,
I watch my day's twilight
    approaching.

The hair's half grey,
The cheeks have lost colour,
I've slowed down.
    The fair's almost over.

The swift rivers and cataracts
I had to cross are behind me.
But I smile when there's no
    canoe I can see.

1940

'Those whose heart's thatch'

Those whose heart's thatch
Hasn't caught fire, never find
The treasures buried there.

Their ambition asleep,
The lamp of frenzy
Is cold inside them,
The sun darkens their sky.

They don't know what's said
In the book of their lives,
Their strings are unswept,
Their music absent.

1941

'There was mist'

There was mist along the pond's edge,
There was a cordon of bluish green leaves,
The mango's branch stretched over the water.
Darkness had pitched its tent,
The place was deserted,
A procession of fireflies went by,
The breeze smelt of the forest,
The coconut trees swayed in sequence,
The date palms stood guard over everything,
The hidden hawk cuckoo sounded its call,
Jackals moved about freely.
Sunrise – and a star glimmered.
Ripples appeared in the pond.
A star shone in the deep.

1943

'By the roadside'

By the roadside
A *paan* shop. In the distance,
An ekka driver thumps his horse
On the rump, an almsman
Blesses a child, a koel calls out
From the pipal, a bullock cart
Crawls along the track.
The blossoming neem fills the air
With its scent. Sunlight
Passing through the sieve of branches
Falls on the ground. To the right,
A tiller drives his team; to the left,
Birds hop in the sand. The rain-tree's
Surface roots are twisty.

1943

'Because there's corn on the cob here'

Because there's corn on the cob here,
The crone is here, the lover is here.
There's a crowd here and an audience,
There are serenades and violins, generosity and bravado,
The flame is here, the moth is here,
Because there's corn on the cob here.

The eye is here, its gaze fixed,
The pulse throbs, the spirit's dead.
The two-eyed is here, the one-eyed is here,
Because there's corn on the cob here.

Mummy is here, daddy is here,
A slap across the cheek and lollipops are here,
The strapping uncle and the old grandfather are here
Because there's corn on the cob here.

1943

Quintet

I

The eyes focused, darkness became light,
The rock salt sweet.

II

The new leader comes through the door.
Expect a sovereign, get a brass farthing.

III

Our men have drowned
Whenever they've stepped on another man's boat.

IV

He paid the land rent;
He blocked the thoroughfare.

V

The stock has arrived, no bidders for it.
Come prepared to fight, no one to fight with.

1944

'Saw dark clouds'

Saw dark clouds in the overcast sky,
Saw lotuses in ponds nodding in the breeze.

The sweet jasmine and the yellow whispered in the ear,
The peacocks danced, the pipal swayed.

A wager laid was taken up at once,
Saw button quails in the pit wrestling like goshawks.

Tillers left for the fields, boys practised holds,
Saw knots of girls singing songs of parting.

[1946]*

*Dates in square brackets are of first book publication.

'The king got away'

The king got away.
He built forts
And raised armies.
His courtiers flattered him,
Anxious for favours;
Brahmins surrounded him,
They'd ensnared the countryside
With their scriptures.
The poets sang his bravery,
The storytellers told tales,
The chroniclers wrote accounts,
The dramatists made adaptations
For the stage.
The court's splendour kept everyone entranced.
The poorest woman behaved like a queen.
Religion was encouraged, so was treachery.
A holy war was fought.
A river of blood flowed.
The people shut their eyes and bathed in it.
Their eyes opened. The king got away.

[1946]

Betrayal

The face yellowed.
The spine curved. The hands folded.
Darkness rose in the eyes.
Centuries went by.
Great sages came, saints came, poets came
And uttered profundities.
    Some said that one is three,
    Others that three is three.
    Some felt the pulse, some admired the lotus,
    Some had a good time, some kissed the fingers.
    The people said, We've been blessed.
But the little tambourine held out.
The mridang split into the tabla,
The vina became the surbahar,
And we now play the piano.
Dawn breaks. The network of rays spreads
And paints the lips of the cardinal points red,
Making them look like harlots at night.
The culture of betrayal has betrayed us.

[1946]

'Don't tie your boat here'

Don't tie your boat here,
My friend, or the whole village
Will come out.
Her laughter rose from these
River-steps, here she sat
In the water and bathed.
Lingering eyes didn't
Easily let go of her;
The legs felt drained
Of all strength.
She said much in that laughter,
Leaving much unsaid;
She listened to the gossip,
Suffered quietly, and gave
Everyone the slip.

January 23, 1950

'Its poison quenched, life's arrow's poised for flight'

Its poison quenched, life's arrow's poised for flight,
The lamp of hope burns in the heart's arbour,
The dark road a thin light-beam hints at,
As the north star in full-starred heaven aids navigation.
Time for dalliance to end, for flowers the hour of withdrawal;
Withering after fruitage or before, they fall
On leaves as sagacious men or common;
From his bed of arrows, Bhishma looks up intently.
Mid-summer's heat relents, the rains too abate,
A soft autumn morning beneath frosted hairlets,
January's bone-chill, the fragrance of mango blossoms in spring.
The game's up for my cardinal-kissing all-weather movent
And caesural craft. Allusion and rhetoric, feeling and harmony,
Elements of style, rules of prosody, slip from my hand,
Playthings turn into embarrassments. Grapplers loosen
Their grip, gone are the days of marksmanship,
Slack is the hide drawn tightly once like a shield.
Another dawning, another turning of the heart's wheel.

SHAKTI CHATTOPADHYAY

'A memory comes back'

A memory comes back.
    The whistle, the junction,
The level crossing, a slow train.
    Will I see you in the window, reading Hart Crane?

The journey was long, a hundred and fifty miles,
    At the end of which all I got is,
'You aren't so rich to be wasting money like this.'
    You were right. I was then just a schoolteacher.

We sat in the moonlight.
    You took out a photograph
And said, 'Keep it.'
    I have it in my wallet.

A memory comes back.
    The whistle, the junction,
The level crossing, a slow train.
    Don't tell me you still read Hart Crane.

It's Not a Very Happy Time, Not a Very Joyful Time

The body shakes all over, walls crash into walls, cornices into cornices,
    The midnight sidewalks change places.
It's the hour of homecoming, home inside home, leg inside leg,
    Ribcage inside ribcage,
And nothing else – or is there? – until one gets home.

The body shakes all over, walls crash into walls, cornices into cornices,
    The midnight sidewalks change places.
It's the hour of homecoming, home inside home, leg inside leg,
    Ribcage inside ribcage,
And nothing else.

'Stop!' And you freeze. Your hands go up,
And you're bundled into a van.
Black Maria inside Black Maria inside Black Maria.
You go past rows of unlit windows, doors, a graveyard, piles of skeletons.
Maggots inside skeletons, life inside maggots, death inside life, and
    therefore
Death inside death
And nothing else.

'Stop!' And you freeze. Your hands go up,
And you get thrown out of one car into another,
Where there is always someone waiting for you,
    tenacious as a banyan tree
Growing in a wall,
Plaster gripped in its green fist.

Unknown to you, hidden like a firm bud behind leaves,
She waits with a garland, the wedding noose,
In her golden spider hands.
Your wedding's at midnight when sidewalks change places –
    The body shakes all over,
Walls crash into walls, cornices into cornices.

Imagine, the train stationary and the platform gaining speed,
A fused electric bulb as bright as starlight;
Imagine, the feet not moving and the sandals walking away,
Heaven where hell is and hell where heaven;
Imagine, newborns carrying the dead in strollers to Nimtala,
And, across the river, old men dancing in the bridal-chamber.

It's not a very happy time, not a very joyful time,
When I come home shaking all over,
Walls crashing into walls, cornices into cornices,
The sidewalks changing places under my feet,
Feet inside feet, ribcage inside ribcage, home inside home,
And nothing else.

The Key

I've preserved the key
    You thought was lost.
How did you open the trunk without it?

Do you still have a mole on your chin?
    Tell me, heart, does travelling help?
Not that it would've kept me from writing this letter.

I don't think I'll keep
    The key much longer.
Write to me if you want it sent.

I remember your face
    Covered with tears.
Write to me if you want it sent.

Zuleika Dobson

Here the great houses,   vast courtyards,   a thousand carriages
        And on the lake golden

Swans lifting their wings.   I must be crazy, Zuleika Dobson,
        To want you still.

The rain-cloud's crest   reddens the north-west,
        A storm's blown down the sal trees.

The moon's just risen.   I await your decision,
        Zuleika Dobson.

Epitaph

He gave up none of the world's pleasures;
He was a poet and a scrounge.

Rejoice! said his publishers. The fellow's dead.
At least he won't now turn up threateningly at the office,
Dressed for the evening, demanding his royalties:
The money, you swine, or I'll gut the place.

And so he was laid on the pyre – poet, troublemaker, pauper.

Vinod Kumar Shukla

'That man put on a new woollen coat and went away like a thought'

That man put on a new woollen coat and went away like a thought.

In rubber flip-flops I struggled behind.

The time was six in the morning, the time of hand-me-downs, and it
    was freezing cold.

Six in the morning was like six in the morning.

There was a man standing under a tree.

In the mist it looked like he was standing inside his own blurred shape.

The blurred tree looked exactly like a tree.

To its right was a blurred horse of inferior stock,

Looking like a horse of inferior stock.

The horse was hungry, the mist like a grassy field to him.

There were other houses, trees, roads, but no other horse.

There was only one horse. I wasn't that horse,

But my breath when I panted was indistinguishable from the mist.

If the man standing at that one spot under the tree was the master,

Then to him I was a horse at a gallop, horseshoes nailed to my boot soles.

1964

'It's like a city built on a dry lakebed'

'It's like a city built on a dry lakebed,' I said to my friend.
A flock of tame ducks
Walked on the left of the road.
There were people arriving all the time.
I'd invoked the names of sailing boats
Before putting on my shoes.
The shoes weren't waterproof.
If I could swim I wouldn't have worn them.
There were many flocks of ducks,
Looking like flocks of men.
This flock of ducks
Was like a duck.
It had a duck's bill and wings.
The duck-like neck, though, was my friend's.
It hung out of his shirt and trousers
As if out of a bag
And would have fitted a man's grip nicely.
It was round in shape.
His shirt pocket was like a second bag.
Smaller in size, it could still hold
Two eggs or the money for two eggs.
My friend was injury prone.
He and I had an argument over egg stalls and fighter jets.

1966

'Turning to the drought'

Turning to the drought in the political dispute,
I kept quiet about the flock of birds
That had risen from the riverbank
Like a wave rising in a thousand fragments.
But pointing to a bird in our midst,
The participants already half asleep,
I raised my voice and said one of the fragments
Had landed on the table.
At once everyone jumped in.
The fragment, they said, had come in
Through the window;
It was perched on a peg in the wall;
They wanted to freshen up, etcetera.
And the wave's face resembles a river.
The face of a bucket of water resembles a river.
With parliament taking the shape of a comb,
The government decided to lose all its hair.

1966

'I don't seem to remember'

I don't seem to remember
There was a flower in the bush,
But I don't see it,
Not even from up close.

What I remember
Is perhaps there was a flower
That was a flower
Even when seen from afar.

From how far? I never came
Even suddenly upon it to guess.
Trying to remember I realize
Just how much I forget.

1978

'A five-year-old girl'

A five-year-old girl,
The youngest in the group,
Came running up to me and said,
Dada, your lady-love is here.

My wife made the visitor
Sit down next to her
But I ran upstairs
Where the other tenant lived.
It was like running
From the terai to the mountains.

And from there I said,
The rent for this place,
From the terai to the mountains,
Is fifty rupees,
Though when I was alone
And there was no one else
Living in this whole province,
The landlord charged thirty.

We just about manage,
My wife said to my lady-love.
We no longer now feel
That we live in a province
But in rented accommodation.

We sweep and mop the floor
Not of a province but of our house.
We're a small family,

A boy and a girl,
And don't have much
To do with the world.

Of course we do, I protested.
The plaster's crumbling
Not of our house but of the province.
The problem's not in our kitchen alone.
Everyone cooks.

My lady-love looked
As though she was hungry.

Even at home I miss my home.

1976

'Seeing Mount Dhaulagiri'

Seeing Mount Dhaulagiri,
I was reminded of its picture,
As I'd seen the picture first.

Among the pictures in my house
Are portraits of my ancestors.
I haven't seen my ancestors,
So whenever I think of them
It's their portraits I think of.

But not after seeing Dhaulagiri.
Now it's the ancestors who come to mind
And not their likenesses.

'My eight-anna coin'

My eight-anna coin
Is lost.
When I look for it
I find a silver rupee.
The rupee isn't mine,
But stamped on it
Is my severed head.
The rest of me must then be
In the eight-anna coin,
And that's why I've been
Desperately looking for it.
How was I to know
That my incomplete person
Would turn into
This money chase?

'This colourful picture'

This colourful picture
Picked up in the bazaar
And hanging on the wall
Is of chubby pink-faced
Children – so unlike our own,
Who're neither as chubby,
Nor as pretty, nor wear
Such nice clothes.

These pictures sell a lot.
There's always someone in every family
Who'll feel as a father feels
And bring one home.

The truth is, though no one says it,
They're all worried about their children.

'The way the sun was going down'

The way the sun was going down
Where it was going down
In the sea, the west was
Going down with it, leaving
No west for tomorrow's sun
To go down in.
May be tomorrow it'll set in some other direction.
In that case, let it.

Where it rises in the sea
The sun is like a sea bird
Trying to rise,
But with the oil on the surface
Sticking to its feathers,
It cannot.

To watch the sunrise that is not a sunrise
There are no tourists
Or tourist souls.

After a whole day of this sunrise
That is not a sunrise,
The sun unable to rise sets.

'This year too in the plains'

This year too in the plains
There are no mountains.
For centuries the mountains have stayed in one place;
It's time they moved.
The Vindhyas, for instance, should come closer
To the bus stand and law courts,
And the Satpura go behind
The village school or farm.
The Himalayas seem unfair
To a place that doesn't have the Himalayas;
This maidan seems unfair
To a place that doesn't have a maidan;
Tatanagar seems unfair
To a place that is not Tatanagar.
This year let this level ground be displaced
Not to the terai but the Himalayas,
The ground's highest point rising like a Himalayan peak.
Let's have Bhopal this year
Near Bakal and Pariyajob,
Varanasi on the banks of the Mahanadi,
Gariaband near the Ganga,
Chandigarh near Sanchi,
Nandgaon near Faridkot,
And Madras next to Moradabad.
All places should be displaced
And brought near all other places,

So that every place is near every other place
And not a single person is displaced
Because of drought, terrorism, or war
From the village this year.

Stroller

My parents go out for a walk.
They are wearing their best clothes,
Made when they got married,
And are pushing a stroller.
I'm sitting in the stroller
And look at the world
With small thirty-five-year-old eyes,
Through thick glasses.
The passers-by laugh,
Talk in whispers,
Or look the other way.
I ask my parents if we can't
Get rid of the stroller.
I may not be steady on my feet,
I may not be able to run
At Olympic speed, but surely,
I say, I can take baby steps.
My parents pucker up their lips.
You are incapable of walking properly,
They say, you will not be able to run,
And at your age no one
Takes baby steps.
We're both quite exhausted.
Still, we sit you in the stroller
And take you out.
Now don't be so inconsiderate,
And stop pestering us.

1983

Black Bag

I have a desire
To put an end to my life,
But not today,
There's nothing special
About today.

Moreover,
I have two glass bottles to clean,
A haircut to get,
My cataracts operated,
Plants to water
(They're flowering at the moment),
A younger sister to look after.
And I haven't stopped dreaming of the stranger
Who'll leave me his millions.

For now I'll put
The talk of death
In my tattered black shopping bag
Full of holes
And hang it from a nail
In the wall.

To be honest,
I'd like to become a sadhu.
But it'll be years before I can bring
Any sort of order to the chaos
That surrounds me.

There's also the awkwardness
Of moving around in a loincloth,
Begging for alms.

That's one thing.
Then, there are the mothers
Who'll want to scare their little ones
By pointing at us:
There goes a sadhu.
He's come to catch you.
It's not easy to get used to all this.

Best that I put this away too
In my tattered black shopping bag
Full of holes
And hang it from a nail
In the wall.

2009

What Paper Likes

The blank sheet of paper
Likes to be scribbled on.

Why else would I bother
To write poems?

2009

Tail

I have two hands, two feet,
Two ears and two eyes.

But the best part is
That there is one nose and two nostrils,
One mouth and thirty-two teeth,
And ... and
Okay, let me tell you then.
There's also this thing that is hanging.

No, there's no tail.
Only monkeys have tails.

2009

Mangalesh Dabral

Woman in Love

The woman in love
Has this dream every night.
What's it about? One morning,
She decides to find out.

Around her she sees the most ordinary things:
Sandy ground,
A tap left running,
Her disarrayed room,
And something she can see
She cannot see, though she looks again.

The woman in love
Trusts no one.
She drops her comb
And turns her back to the mirror.
She says, I'm okay as I am.

One by one her friends desert her.
The sun goes down, keeping its distance.
The wind blows, but not through her hair.
The table is cleared
Without her having eaten.

The woman in love
Is deceived every day.
She doesn't know what's happening outside,
Who the cheat is, who takes her for a ride.
She doesn't know how it all began.

The world's a child in my arms,
Says the woman in love.
She comes out on the road alone
And looks at the big city around her.
Somewhere or other, she says, I'll find a place to live.

The Quiet House

The sun by slow degrees warms up the walls,
A low fire burns nearby,
There's a ball lying on the bed,
The books are silent,
Countless tales of adversity hidden in them.

I'm half awake, half asleep,
Listening to outside sounds,
No one crying,
No one threatening or pleading,
No one praying,
No one begging for alms.

And there's no bitterness in me,
Just some empty space
For someone to come and fill,
Nor do I feel helpless,
But an ache spreads through my body
As I recall the house of my childhood,
In whose courtyard, lying on my stomach,
I'd take the sun.

I ask nothing of the world,
And can live as squirrels do,
As grass does, or a ball,

Not at all worried
That at any moment someone can shake this house
And bring it down.

Poem of Dreams

There's no running away from dreams; they happen as a consequence of waking. They tell us what we were and what we shall become. They make our half lives whole. While we breathlessly rush about one hemisphere, they keep us quietly asleep in a corner of the other.

In dreams the earth looks round, just as our schoolbooks had said. The sun's heat is intense and stars shiver in their cold light. Trees of happiness grow around us. Someone on a bicycle goes by; we hear a radio playing. We see our roots immersed in clear water. We see the moon shining in a small dark room.

In dreams we see ourselves as righteous men. We see an old cracked mirror. We see blood coming out of our noses.

Poem of Paper

One day we find sheets of paper that were once important scattered everywhere around us. We see them even as we go to sleep. They put an end to our dreams and cause insomnia. Our everyday lives, the things we hate to admit to ourselves, are buried in them. Which is why, much as we'd like to, we cannot even sell them to the rag-and-bottle man. We have no choice except to sit down and destroy them.

This is how old letters get torn, written by sympathetic friends when we were down and out. Declarations of unrequited love, along with the poems by some major poets, poems we believed would remove the world's hunger, get reduced to shreds. Now you cannot even make a paper boat or missile with them, the kind that flies a short distance and turns back.

We have become wordless, and all but lost our speech. We go on tearing the paper. It's our only hope.

Notes

Distance in Statute Miles
'*Company Period*': The details are from Stuart Cary Welch, *A Flower from Every Meadow: Indian Paintings from American Collections* (1973).

Middle Earth
'*The World's a Printing-House*': The title is from Francis Quarles, *Divine Fancies* (1632), IV, iii.

'*Location*': The book referred to is D.W. Robertson, *A Preface to Chaucer: Studies in Medieval Perspective* (1962).

'*Disiecti Membra Poetae*': The title is from Horace, *Satires*, I, iv, 62.

Songs of Kabir
KG 170: The shaven-headed men are the *Nath-panthi*s, belonging to a religious sect of the Hatha Yoga school. Several reasons have been given for the practice of smearing the body with ashes. 'They signify death to the world . . . or they may indicate that the body must be reduced to ashes ultimately, or they may be a sign that the Yogi has abandoned the world.' (G.W. Briggs, *Gorakhnath and the Kanphata Yogis*, 1938, pp. 16–17).

KG 174: John Stratton Hawley and Mark Jurgensmeyer, who have translated this poem in *Songs of the Saints of India* (1988), say in a note, 'The practices of wandering naked, shaving the head, and learning to retain the semen all pertain to yoga in some form' (p. 185). The first two stanzas of the poem are almost identical with those by Saraha, written half a millennium earlier: 'If going naked means release / then the dog and the jackal / must have it; / if baldness is perfection / then a young girl's bottom / must have it' (Roger R. Jackson, *Tantric Treasures: Three Collections of Mystical Verse from Buddhist India*, 2004, p. 56).

KG 182: In the original, the caste mark is specified: '*teeni dandi*' or 'three lines'. The lines 'refer to the *tridandi* or *tripunda*, the three horizontal lines traced on the forehead of a Shaivite Brahman at the time of his initiation' (Charlotte Vaudeville, *A Weaver Named Kabir*, 1993, p. 218). On circumcision Vaudeville says, 'Kabir was strongly opposed to circumcision. The gibe at that Muslim practice suggests that low-caste converts to Islam such as the Julahas resented the practice which orthodox Muslims tried to enforce on them' (p. 219).

KG 129: What has here been translated as 'walking mosque' is, in the original, a 'mosque with ten doors', the ten doors being the nine holes of the human body and '(in yoga) the opening at the top of the skull through which the soul is said to escape to union with the absolute, or in death' (*Oxford Hindi–English Dictionary*).

KG 84: In the original, the paradise is *baikuntha*, 'or the Paradise of delights which is supposed to be the residence of god Vishnu' (Vaudeville, *A Weaver Named Kabir*, p. 265).

KG 160: In his essay 'Men, Women, and Saints', A.K. Ramanujan calls saints the 'third gender': 'Just as the male saint-to-be drops his caste, wealth, and intelligence, he finally drops his masculinity, becomes a woman, so that he can be open to the lord. The male saint yearns to achieve a woman's state in his society, so he can yearn for and couple with god – to accept the feminine side of himself, as Jung would say, shedding his machismo.' Women saints similarly 'may take on the characteristics of men: they leave the house questing for their personal god (not their husband's or father's) and a community of their own choosing' (*The Collected Essays of A.K. Ramanujan*, 1999, pp. 290–91).

KG 62: Yama, the Lord of Death, is sometimes represented as carrying an iron rod in one hand and a noose in the other.

Uncollected Translations

Nirala was the pen-name of Suryakant Tripathi (1899–1961). His family was from the Kannauj region of Uttar Pradesh but migrated to the small princely state of Mahishadal in Bengal, where his father was a court official. Nirala published novels, short stories, and books of essays, in addition to a dozen volumes of poetry. He is widely seen as the greatest Hindi poet after Tulsi Das in the 16th century.

Its poison quenched: Widely regarded as Nirala's last poem, it was written weeks before his death in October 1961.

Bhishma: In the *Mahabharata*, Bhishma sides with the Kauravas against the Pandavas and is killed by Arjuna, who shot so many arrows into him that 'when he fell from his chariot he was upheld from the ground by the arrows and lay as on a couch of darts' (J. Dowson, *Hindu Classical Dictionary*)

After Tagore and Jibhananda Das, **Shakti Chattopadhyay** (1933–1995) was the most loved Bengali poet of his time. When he won the Sahitya Akademi award in 1983 for *Jete pari kintu kano jabo* (I Can Leave But Why Should I), his 40 books were said to have sold some 1,200,000 copies. In the 1960s he befriended Allen Ginsberg in Calcutta, and his influence on Bengali poetry, clearing it of the 'fog of punditry', was in many ways similar to Ginsberg's in America.

Vinod Kumar Shukla was born in Rajnandgaon, in central India, in 1937. For most of his working life he taught at Indira Gandhi Agricultural University, Raipur,. His first full-length collection in Hindi was mysteriously titled *Voh* *aadami chala gaya naya naya garam coat pahankar vichar ki tarah* (That Man Put on a New Woollen Coat and Went Away Like a Thought, 1981). He writes poems of great simplicity, whose wordplay and syntactical shifts make them difficult to follow and sometimes impossible to translate.

Pavankumar Jain (1947–2013) studied at Bombay University and the National Institute of Design, Ahmedabad. He wrote in English and Gujarati, and while still a student started the little magazine *Tornado* (1967–71). His only collection of Gujarati poems, *Pasath kavyo* (Sixty-five Poems), appeared a year before his death. He observed the minutiae of everyday life, and it little affected the steadfastness with which he looked that the life observed was often not another's but his own.

Mangalesh Dabral (1948–2020) was born in a village in the Garhwal Himalayas, but for the last 45 years of his life he lived in Delhi. He published five books of poems and two collections of essays in Hindi. 'My poetry was born among mountains, lived among the stones,' he said, 'but soon it migrated to the cities where the world was not so simple and innocent despite all its attractions.' Dabral died in the 2020 pandemic.